T0068746

H.G. WELLs

FIRST CITIZEN OF THE FUTURE

KEITH FERRELL

M Evans

Lanham • New York • Boulder • Toronto • Plymouth, UK

M. Evans
An imprint of The Rowman & Littlefield Publishing Group, Inc.
4501 Forbes Boulevard, Suite 200, Lanham, Maryland 20706
http://www.rlpgtrade.com

10 Thornbury Road, Plymouth PL6 7PP, United Kingdom

Distributed by National Book Network

Copyright © 1983 Keith Ferrell
First Rowman & Littlefield paperback edition 2014

All rights reserved. No part of this book may be reproduced in any form or by any electronic or mechanical means, including information storage and retrieval systems, without written permission from the publisher, except by a reviewer who may quote passages in a review.

British Library Cataloguing in Publication Information Available

Library of Congress Cataloging-in-Publication Data Available

ISBN 13: 978-1-59077-356-7 (pbk: alk. paper)

♻™ The paper used in this publication meets the minimum requirements of American National Standard for Information Sciences—Permanence of Paper for Printed Library Materials, ANSI/NISO Z39.48-1992.

Printed in the United States of America

CONTENTS

FOR MY FATHER

ONE

THE PROPER ORDER OF SOCIETY

THE DUSTY CHINA SHOP was named Atlas House, and it rested the burden of its world on the shoulders of Sarah Wells. She did not carry the weight well. Atlas House stood on High Street in Bromley, a London suburb, and its surroundings, contents, and customers drove Sarah into depression, sometimes despair. Everything and everyone on High Street seemed to Sarah either garish or grimy or both. She loathed the street and she loathed her house. Her rightful place was in the lovely estates of the wealthy, working as a trusted employee in the midst of culture, beauty, and grace. Instead, she was trapped in this three-story box, many of whose stairs lacked carpeting, most of whose walls reeked of the paraffin used to battle, unsuccessfully, bugs.

It was 1866 and Sarah had lived in Atlas House for eleven years. She had raised her two boys in this house. And here she had lost her only daughter, Frances, barely two years before. Sarah thought often of Frances, that perfect little girl. Her daughter. She'd taught Frances so much, had given her all the benefits she was able. Frances was only nine when she died, just coming to understand Sarah's explanations of the proper order of society, the order of society in which Sarah and her husband, Joseph, once held and then lost their place.

The proper order of society. That order was a rigid class

system, the essence of English life, a living link with history. According to the rules of society, privilege and rank were determined by the class into which one was born. The origins of the class system lay in the Middle Ages, a time when the king was served by his knights, who pledged him their allegiance and skills as warriors. The knights, in turn, held their place above vassals and serfs. Even the vassals and serfs had their own ranks among themselves.

Over the centuries this idea of order in English society remained well established, although its nature changed and evolved. The warrior knight, whose sword was no longer needed to defend the land, became known as a gentleman. These gentlemen retained not only the great tracts of land that had been in their families since medieval times, but also the highest position, other than that of royalty itself, in English society.

Below the gentlemen were those who served them. As England moved from an agricultural to an industrial economy, the class of vassals and serfs gave way to the rising middle class. The majority of the population was no longer needed to work the fields. Industry was drawing more and more people to the cities, where their great hope was of advancement, of getting ahead.

There were strict limits to how far one could advance. A person born into the middle or lower classes could never become a true gentleman or lady. But, as Sarah Wells believed, one could improve one's self within the boundaries of one's own class. This was the great goal of Sarah's life.

Sarah herself had been educated, a rare accomplishment for an innkeeper's daughter born in 1823. Sarah's education was neither broad nor deep—she could read and write, and had been exposed to a few other subjects—but it gave her a sense of confidence and made her feel that she was special. With her talents she was sure she would find her own secure place in society's proper order.

Following a brief apprenticeship to a dressmaker, Sarah

found her proper place. She became a lady's maid, working in fine houses, serving those better-born than she. It was a position she enjoyed, took seriously, and felt proud of. She served her mistresses perfectly, and one of them, Miss Fetherstonhaugh, came to think of Sarah as a friend. Sarah took much pleasure from her status, and left service only to care for her ailing mother. Sarah's parents died during the same season in 1853. Before that year was out, before securing another position, Sarah married Joseph Wells, a gardener.

Joseph Wells was a short man, physically strong and attractive. He was well employed as head gardener of a large estate. In addition to being respectable, proper enough for Sarah's idea of things, the job carried a handsome salary and brought with it a pleasant cottage into which the young couple settled. Joseph enjoyed his work: He was a vigorous outdoorsman who derived great satisfaction from making things grow. With such a bright future, Sarah felt very happy and soon was expecting a child.

But while the couple was happy, Joseph's employer was not. Joseph did not take well to instructions; he had his own idea of how things should be done. His temper flashed too often. In February 1855 Frances was born. In July Joseph lost his job. For the rest of her life Sarah would seethe with bitterness over this cruel twist of fate.

Unemployed, with prospects bleak, Joseph turned from service to the world of commerce. He applied his meager savings and a small inheritance to the purchase of Atlas House from a cousin. The shop was not a success, despite the strength in its name. Few of its china pieces matched, and even fewer found buyers. There was little money for expanding or improving the inventory. Sarah began her descent into self-pity not long after moving into Atlas House. She felt that her hard-won place in the proper order was lost. She felt that she and Joseph had been cheated by Joseph's cousin, and cheated by life itself.

The management of Atlas House, not only as a home but

also as a business, was left almost entirely to Sarah. Joseph, always athletic, became increasingly involved in cricket, playing with several clubs. He supplemented the dreary income from china with a line of cricket equipment, which earned slightly brighter receipts. Joseph rarely remained at home, and when he did he could always be found lounging in front of the store, talking with his cronies. Most of Sarah's time was spent in the kitchen, a small, poorly lighted cubicle in the basement of Atlas House. So determined was Joseph to leave the duties of business to Sarah that he rigged a signaling device by which he could summon her from the basement when a customer entered the shop.

Even while her marriage was collapsing, Sarah bore two more children. Both were boys: Frank, born in 1857, and Fred, born in 1862. Each pregnancy was a dreaded burden to Sarah, each child a trial. Still, she endeavored to instill in her sons the same knowledge of society's order that she had taught her daughter.

1866 found Sarah expecting again. This pregnancy took a greater toll on her than any of the others. During the summer she prayed for her misery soon to be over.

On September 21, 1866, Sarah's prayers were answered. She gave birth to her final child, another boy. She named the baby Herbert George Wells. Bertie, as she called him and as he was known throughout childhood, was Sarah's last great hope for the future. She wanted to make him into the perfect child her daughter had been.

A third son made little difference in Joseph Wells's habits. He remained away from the house for long periods, playing cricket for badly needed money, sometimes simply staying away. Sarah's burdens increased. She fought her despair by spoiling Bertie. Anything the child wanted was his. He was fawned over, coddled, and petted, a situation that would result in his being labeled a sissy in school.

Bertie learned rapidly that the special attention he received increased with his ability to perform special feats. He memorized songs, sayings, drew pictures with a skill beyond his years. At every gathering of the family Bertie held the center of attention.

Bertie was a small child and lacked his father's healthy constitution. However, he possessed a vivid imagination and a keen sense of what he wanted. By the time he was old enough to walk Bertie understood that he, through his temper, could control the entire house. He used that temper to full advantage. He cried and screamed if his brothers so much as touched one of his toys. He was equally loud in his demands that he be allowed to play with their belongings. Sarah always conceded to Bertie's desires—if he wanted to play with Fred's and Frank's toys he could.

When Bertie's outbursts became too much for Fred and Frank to bear, they dragged him to the attic, where they took turns smothering him with heavy pillows. They held the pillows over Bertie's face until he nearly blacked out. In later years the youngest of the Wells boys would reminisce wonderingly that his brothers did not kill him.

But Bertie did survive the smotherings and the other traumas of childhood. He watched as his brothers were both apprenticed as draper's assistants. Draper's stores sold cloth and other merchandise; in America such stores were known as dry-goods stores. A draper's assistant was a very junior clerk. It was a job that Sarah Wells found appealing, for he sons, and all draper's assistants, wore formal black morning coats and catered to customers from the better levels of society. It was a respectable beginning for a young man, a start in the middle class, and it was the destiny she wanted for Bertie.

But Bertie soon discovered that there were other things in life than toys and the proper order of society.

He was seven and playing with a group of boys. One of them playfully tossed small Bertie into the air, but Bertie twisted during his descent and missed being caught. He came down on a tent peg and was overcome with agony.

His leg was broken.

In old age Herbert George Wells would look back on the day of the accident as the luckiest day of his life.

Despite the pain—and in 1874 the method of setting a broken leg consisted of simple splints strapped together with no treatment of the swelling—Bertie found that there were certain benefits to being an invalid. He was put to convalesce on the living room couch. That large room soon became his private kingdom. He could ask for anything he wanted—even beyond his previous demands. Bertie received candy and other sweets, pencils, toys, coloring books, anything.

Mostly Bertie asked for books.

On that couch, in the living room, between his seventh and eighth birthdays, Bertie Wells discovered reading.

Sarah had taught Bertie his letters at an early age. The two of them would spell such words as *butter* in the steamed-up windows of the kitchen during winter. But Sarah felt that the great reason to learn to read was to be able to study the Bible and those religious books of which she approved. Sarah was a devoutly, piously religious woman. She was an Anglican, but her family had been members of a very strict sect. Those beliefs stayed with her throughout her life, and she taught Bertie and his brothers of a terrifying and vengeful God, a God who wreaked punishment on those who sinned. She showed Bertie a variety of religious pamphlets, all of them illustrated with terrifying pictures of the perils in store for sinners.

As Bertie recovered from his broken leg, however, he learned that books offered other lessons than those that Sarah's pamphlets held. Years later he would recall mastering the technique of "leaving my body to sit impassive in a crumpled up attitude in a chair or sofa, while I wandered over the hills and far away in novel company and new scenes." For Bertie this was magic. In books he could leave far behind the dingy confines of Atlas House, the troubles between his parents, his own smallness. He felt as though his world were growing faster than he could keep up. Bertie Wells surrounded himself with books and attacked them so ferociously that later he could barely recall their titles. At that time he had no interest in authors and ignored the names on the title page. He sought only the print-filled pages of the books themselves, for on those pages he found wonders.

He discovered worlds far beyond Atlas House and High Street. There were thousands of these other worlds, an infinite supply, all neatly printed and illustrated with the most magnificent pictures. Bertie traveled all over the globe through a two-volume world geography; in those books he met Indians and Eskimos, whalers and savages. He learned of fearsome animals, such as gorillas and tigers. Another book made him aware of astronomy, of the awesome size and complexity of the universe. Biographies let him make the acquaintance of the duke of Wellington, history books taught him of the recently ended American Civil War, science books gave him the first hints of the mystery of evolution.

These were not simple children's books. Among the volumes Bertie devoured was a collection of *Punch,* a British humor magazine whose most favored targets were the political leaders of the day. *Punch* and similar magazines sparked in young Bertie Wells a fascination with politics that would stay with him throughout his life.

By the time his leg was healed Bertie had become addicted to reading. He could not put down a book until it was finished, and then, as likely as not, he would immediately open another one. His parents did not fully approve of this obsession, although Joseph Wells himself had a strong love of literature. There was, however, nothing to be done about Bertie and his books. Herbert George Wells was a Reader.

When Bertie was healed, Sarah decided it was time for

him to attend school. Sarah saw education as a right for her children by virtue of their class. Her own education had been a rarity for the times, but years had passed since then and the times had changed. England was the world's greatest industrial nation, its cities were bulging, and with the shift in population away from agriculture it became obvious to the government that some sort of plan had to be made for universal education. An uneducated populace simply could not do the work of the modern age; one did not need to know how to read to push a plow, but illiterates were handicapped in factories. Certain basics—reading and simple math—were necessary if only to keep industrial production high. The Elementary Education Act of 1871 organized England's school system into a unified whole, or at least was a major step in that direction.

Sarah, though, wanted no part of public schools for her Bertie. The boy had for a time attended a small school near Atlas House when he was five, and now, at the age of seven, he was enrolled in the Bromley Academy, a private school operated by Thomas Morley.

Bromley Academy was a one-room school on High Street, not too far from Atlas House. The purpose of the academy was to prepare young people for a future in the merchant trade, exactly the sort of future to which Sarah had apprenticed Bertie's brothers. At Bromley Academy students learned writing, arithmetic, and a certain amount of history. Morley deliberately modeled his school on the example of higher-class schools attended by the children of gentlemen and ladies. This may have been part of the academy's attraction for Sarah Wells, but in truth Morley's modeling was not successful. Bertie would remember Bromley Academy less as a place of learning than as a room in which Thomas Morley inflicted his moods and prejudices upon his students.

Thomas Morley had in common with Sarah Wells the attitude that life had treated him unfairly. He was not a learned man, and he did not pass on to his students a love of learning. Morley often dozed in class, sleeping at his desk while his students made fun of him. When he awoke, Morley would attack the students, punishing them, driving them non-stop through an hour or two of bookkeeping and clerking. His goal was to turn out suitable employees for the many firms in the area.

If Morley did not transmit a love of learning for its own sake, he did communicate a belief in certain fundamental truths, a passion for order and clarity. Where Sarah's order was that of society and God, Morley taught that the proper order of grammar and mathematics was the key to a successful life. Bertie embraced these ideas of order far more enthusiastically than he had the lessons offered by his mother, and Morley came to take a special interest in the young Wells boy. Bertie did so well in bookkeeping that, during his time at Bromley Academy, he tied for first place as the best bookkeeping student in England.

In other ways the education at Bromley left much to be desired. Morley had little interest in reading for pleasure, in books or study for its own sake. Everything must be a step toward a successful career as a clerk. Bertie, on the other hand, continued to read, expanding his personal horizons beyond the limited ones offered by Morley and Bromley Academy.

Among the worlds Bertie created for himself in his imagination was a world brought to order through his own military leadership. Even as a boy he dreamed of imposing his views on the entire world, just as he imposed his demands on all of Atlas House.

Not only did Bertie daydream while enrolled at Bromley Academy, he also took his first steps toward his future career, his real career. He recorded some of his fantasies on paper. He wrote a children's story called *The Desert Daisy*. It was filled with imaginary royalty, countries, and battles. Bertie even composed his own reviews for the story. All of the reviews were favorable.

When Bertie was eleven another broken leg would alter his life almost as dramatically as the fracture that confined him to the couch when he was seven. This time, however, the broken leg belonged to Joseph Wells, and it served to end a period in the life of the Wells family.

In October 1877 Joseph Wells climbed a ladder to prune the grapevine that grew in the small courtyard at Atlas House. To reach the highest vines Joseph had to balance the ladder on an unsteady bench. The ladder fell and Joseph badly broke his leg.

Joseph was confined to bed for weeks, and unlike his son was unable to escape his misfortune through books. Debts mounted rapidly, and it was obvious that Joseph would no longer be able to play cricket. Without the income brought by the sport, the Wells family soon fell upon hard times. Their diet consisted of bread and cheese. Mr. Morley went unpaid for long periods. Bertie's brother Frank had to contribute, from his small salary as a draper's assistant, the money to buy new shoes for Bertie.

Still, Sarah did what she could to bring in enough money to keep Bertie in school. His education and the launching of him as a proper draper's assistant were her primary concerns. What little affection she may have felt for Bertie's father soon disappeared under the pressure of bills and the anxiety about the future.

Sarah's concern for Bertie's education vanished when Bertie was fourteen. That year, 1880, Sarah was called by Miss Fetherstonhaugh to return to service. It was as though "a great light shone on Mrs. Sarah Wells," her son recalled later.

That great light evidently blinded her to Bertie's desires for the future. Sarah, upon hearing Miss Fetherstonhaugh's offer, immediately began searching for a job into which she could apprentice Bertie. As far as Sarah was concerned, Bertie's education was suddenly complete. He soon found himself apprenticed to the firm of Rodgers and Denyer, a large draper's establishment not far from Windsor Castle.

As for Sarah Wells, she turned her back on Atlas House, Joseph Wells, and her sons. At the age of fifty-seven she returned to service. She, at last, had regained her position in the proper order of society.

TWO
DRAPER

Bertie Wells learned quickly that whatever he was meant for in life, it was not the position of draper's assistant. He loathed the job from the first day and immediately set to searching for ways to escape it.

Rodgers and Denyer was a large drapery emporium, its walls lined with bolts of expensive cloth, shelves filled with buttons and yarn and the other goods the firm sold. It was the job of the draper's assistants to wait on customers, show them samples of merchandise, put the stock back in order after the customer left, and keep account of all money taken in. But these were only the duties the assistants were responsible for during store hours. They had other jobs as well.

Bertie and the other assistants rose early. They had to be on the job by seven-thirty each morning. Between seven-thirty and eight-thirty Bertie cleaned windows, dusted, and prepared himself for the routine of the day's work. Breakfast, at eight-thirty, was simply bread and butter. Work continued, with brief lunch and tea breaks, until eight-thirty at night, when dinner was served.

It was a long day, and there were few moments when the boys could catch their breath. Even the closing of the store each evening offered no respite—the shop had to be swept out and thoroughly cleaned before dinner was served.

Draper's assistants lived either in dormitories on the premises or at home with their parents. Since Sarah Wells had returned to service, Bertie had no home at which to live. He settled into the dormitory at Rodgers and Denyer.

The boys lived several to a room. The lights were extinguished promptly at ten-thirty each night, scarcely two hours after the evening meal. Those two hours were all the time Bertie had to himself each day.

For the privilege of having her son enter this career, Sarah Wells had paid Rodgers and Denyer a fee of fifty pounds, which at that time was the equivalent of several hundred dollars.

Bertie did not pay much attention to his duties. The hours of endless errands, folding neatly and returning cloth to its proper spot after being shown to a customer, cleaning and straightening, and above all the *politeness* that was required of young drapers, did not agree with him. He sought the same sorts of escape he had taken such pleasure from as a child. He left his body to its duties while he let his imagination soar. Unfortunately, while a broken leg will heal while the mind wanders, dusting and accounting do not take care of themselves.

Despite all his abilities and awards as a bookkeeper, Bertie had absolutely no interest in that aspect of his apprenticeship. He was more likely to be found with his nose in a book of higher mathematics than in his ledger. Often he was sloppy with his figures, entering incorrect sums, giving out wrong amounts of change. More than once he just abandoned his tasks and retreated to a hiding place behind a stack of merchandise.

It became inevitable that Bertie's employers would catch up with the young man's negligence. Bertie Wells did not care about his job, and cared less for satisfying the expectations of Rodgers and Denyer.

Finally the day of reckoning arrived. The imbalance in Bertie's books brought him to the edge of being accused of thievery. A cousin who lived nearby interceded, persuading Rodgers and Denyer that Bertie was sloppy and disorganized, but not a thief. This was true. In later years Wells reflected that some other draper's assistant could easily have taken advantage of Bertie's negligence and gotten away with the money.

Rodgers and Denyer dismissed Herbert George Wells as "not refined enough" to be a draper.

Another cousin took Bertie's fate into his hands. Alfred Williams headed a small school in the village of Wookey. "Uncle Williams," as he was known, knew of Bertie's achievements at Bromley Academy, and offered the boy the position of pupil-teacher at the village school.

The position of pupil-teacher required Bertie to teach younger students those subjects he'd already mastered while he proceeded with his own more advanced studies. Most pupil-teachers in England went on to training colleges, where they learned more of the craft of teaching. This became Bertie's great dream.

At the school in Wookey he discovered "that it was pleasanter to stand in front of a class and distribute knowledge ... than sit at a desk or hover behind a counter." Bertie began to consider teaching as his profession.

Unfortunately, Alfred Williams had falsified his credentials in order to become headmaster of the school. When the authorities discovered the lie, Williams was fired. After only a brief period of hope, Bertie's future once more became uncertain.

After staying for a time with relatives, Bertie traveled to Up Park, the fine estate in Sussex, in southeastern England, of which Sarah Wells was the housekeeper.

At Up Park, waiting for another opportunity, Bertie found a good many things to occupy his time. He arrived at the estate just before Christmas, and the huge house bustled with activity in preparation for the holiday. Bertie found he was the source of much amusement for the staff of the house. When a heavy snowfall isolated Up Park, Bertie prepared and distributed a humorous daily newspaper, *The Up Park Alarmist*. He also built a box theater for shadow shows as well as devising other forms of entertainment.

When not entertaining the staff, Bertie remained in the upstairs room that Miss Fetherstonhaugh provided for him. Next to his bedroom was the attic itself, in which were stored many objects that attracted Bertie's attention. He found a variety of books and portfolios of paintings, which he pored over eagerly. He came upon a box of copper pieces that obviously were meant to be screwed together. Bertie did so and was delighted to discover that the pieces assembled as an antique telescope and tripod. He passed many hours with the telescope, aiming it at distant celestial objects, studying the craters of the moon. His mother caught him one night, Bertie's window wide open despite the bitter cold. The chance of becoming sick seemed a minor risk compared to the delights of astronomy, Bertie felt.

Most wonderful of all was the willingness of the Fetherstonhaugh family to let Bertie use the estate's library. He carried volume after volume to his room and read with the same excitement and vigor he'd felt as an injured child. The difference now was in the books he read. The Fetherstonhaugh library contained books by the world's foremost philosophers and writers. Bertie discovered the uncensored *Gulliver's Travels* and found that the children's version he'd read previously only hinted at the richness of that work. He read Plato and Tom Paine, continuing his fascination with the world of politics. He struggled over the French of Voltaire. He was ecstatic.

Such happiness could not last forever. Sarah Wells would not permit it. Bertie's proper place, she felt, was in the mercantile trade, and she set herself the task of finding another position for her son. She soon succeeded, apprenticing Bertie to Samuel Cowpap, a pharmacist in Midhurst.

Bertie was happier in the drugstore than he'd been at Rodgers and Denyer. After all, there was something almost scientific about the pharmacy and its contents. Here Bertie learned to sell medicine, and watched as Mr. Cowpap mixed remedies for all manner of illnesses. The drugstore stocked medicines for veterinarians as well as physicians.

There was also, of course, the less agreeable task of dusting the many bottles, as well as cleaning and shelving and all the other menial chores expected of any apprentice. But on the whole Bertie found the job much more rewarding than that of draper's assistant.

And there was one aspect of the pharmacy apprenticeship that was simply wonderful. This was the study of Latin. Since pharmacy apprentices were expected to pursue a career in the profession, they had to learn Latin, the language of chemistry. Latin had not been offered at Bromley Academy, so Bertie arranged to take lessons from the headmaster of Midhurst Grammar School, Mr. Horace Byatt.

It quickly became obvious to Mr. Byatt that Bertie Wells was an exceptional student. Within four or five hours of study Bertie was already farther advanced in Latin skills than were many of Byatt's full-time students after an entire year. Bertie thought of Latin as something he had not known existed, and at the same time as something that was exactly right for him, so right that it almost seemed he had been waiting for it. He saw immediately the improvement Latin made in his command of English.

Again, though, Bertie had entered an apprenticeship doomed to a short life. After barely a month it grew obvious that Sarah Wells could not afford the fees required of pharmacy apprentices. And so Bertie was once again without employment.

One fortunate experience did come from the collapse of this potential career. It was inconvenient for Bertie to return to Up Park, but Mr. Cowpap had nonetheless evicted Bertie upon learning of the boy's inability to continue as an apprentice. With nowhere to go, Bertie and his mother arranged for him to become a student at Midhurst Grammar School. In February 1881, at the age of fourteen, Bertie Wells was once again a full-time student.

Headmaster Byatt soon discovered that Bertie was as eager to approach and master any subject as he had shown himself to be with Latin. Since Byatt received government financial rewards for the progress of his students, he turned Bertie loose on as many different subjects as the boy could manage. Byatt pointed Bertie in the direction of books, and let Bertie pursue subjects and encounter new ones on his own. Young Bertie moved rapidly through such diverse courses as physiology, mathematics, and others, all coming easily to him.

In later years Wells would look back upon his younger self, reflecting upon the experiences that in less than two years had taken him from Atlas House to draper's assistant to Up Park to pharmacist's apprentice and back to school. For many people such a rush of different experiences would be frightening, disorienting, perhaps overwhelming. Bertie was not deterred. Every new experience enlarged his life, stretched his mind. He came to think that those two years "above all others were the years in which the immediate realities about me began to join on in a rational way to that varied world with which books had acquainted me." He began to see patterns, to understand that the world of books could serve as a map toward mastering the real world, and that experience in the real world was also invaluable and enriching when approaching the world of books. They reinforced each other. Bertie Wells was growing up.

His happiness could not last. His mother was determined to see him well established in a profession suitable for a young man of his class. She soon succeeded in finding another position for her son. While Bertie devoured books and reveled in the study of science, Sarah arranged, through an associate of Miss Fetherstonhaugh's, for Bertie to become a draper's assistant at the Southsea Drapery Emporium.

Draper's assistant once more! It was almost too cruel a fate after only six wonderful weeks as a student at Midhurst. Bertie fought with his mother over the position, but she begged him to try once more to fit into the role of proper young man. Bertie gave in, but as he again took up the dreary duties of draper's assistant his mind seethed with plans for escape.

He feared that if he did not get away from Southsea he would be trapped forever as a merchant's clerk. It was not a bad profession, and certainly preferable to the destitution that was the lot of many young men who could not find jobs, but Bertie wanted more. He knew that he possessed a fine mind and he wanted the opportunity to use it, to expand it, to accomplish serious mental work, not merely to count change and guide his hands as he dusted shelves.

Once employed by Southsea, though, and despite his dreams of escape, Bertie sought to become a good apprentice. The routine was much the same as that at Rodgers and Denyer: early awakening followed by cleaning and preparation for a day of business. Only after the shop was in order was breakfast served. Through the long day Bertie spent his time tending the stocks of material.

Years later he could still recall the many types of cloth. He was responsible for cloths labeled "Hard Book or Turkey Twill . . . rolls of grey and black silesia, flannels . . . a perplexing range of longcloths and calicoes, endless packages of diaper table-cloths . . . rolls of crash, house cloth, ticking and the like . . . ginghams and sateens, cretonne and kindred fabrics." The names were interesting but the materials themselves did not interest Bertie. He felt far more baffled by the variety of cloths than by the structure of Latin grammar.

It was not simply the variety of cloths. Each cloth had to be refolded carefully after each customer's inspection, heavy blankets had to be packed perfectly. Lace curtains drove Bertie to distraction.

The only respite he received during the working day was an occasional errand, during which Bertie loitered and dawdled as much as he dared.

At night, at least, he could read. His employer, Mr. Hyde, held a more liberal attitude about his apprentices' education than did most merchants. Mr. Hyde provided a variety of reading matter for the boys apprenticed to him. There were religious pamphlets, encyclopedias, and scholarly volumes. Bertie took full advantage of the books and often read when he should have been working. The pattern of inattentiveness that had gotten him into so much trouble at Rodgers and Denyer was coming back to the surface at Hyde's Southsea Drapery Emporium.

Despite the better conditions at Southsea—not only were there books, but also the dining room and food were more pleasant—Bertie's resolve to do better as an apprentice soon faded. He came to remember himself at Southsea as an "unwilling worker," often chastised by his employers. Their criticisms stayed with him throughout the years.

"Come up!"

"Oh, look sharp!"

"What in heaven are you doing now?"

"Wells? What is Wells doing? Where on earth is that boy now?"

Upon hearing these questions Bertie would burst into activity for a few minutes. But soon he was daydreaming again or hiding behind a stack of merchandise, his nose deep in a thick book.

Thinking back on this experience, Wells as an adult saw his employers' criticisms as instructive rather than cruel. His supervisors, he came to understand, actually wanted the best for him, wanted him to understand the importance of discipline and a job well done. Nor was Bertie's negligence a product of snobbishness. He did not feel he was better than the more industrious apprentices, he only knew that he was different. Just how different became clear as his employers realized, and made Bertie realize, that he was not meant to be a draper.

Still, Bertie stayed on. By the time he was sixteen he had been at Southsea for more than a year, and was given the responsibility of waiting on customers. He was as poor at that task as he was at all others. Often the change he gave was incorrect, he could not wrap packages, he could not do anything properly.

But he was trapped. He knew that Southsea was probably his last chance as an apprentice. If he failed here where could he go? Become a beggar? Live in the gutter?

In counterpoint to those fears, though, was a voice in the back of his mind. A voice that grew louder each day.

Get out of this trade before it is too late, the voice told him. At any cost get out of it.

But where to? another voice asked.

The answer came during a discussion of Latin with a friend. Headmaster Byatt and Midhurst Grammar School! Why hadn't he thought of it before? Bertie wrote to Byatt and inquired about the possibility of employment as a pupil-teacher.

Byatt responded with cautious optimism. Bertie was now nearly seventeen, too old, really, to be a pupil-teacher. But the headmaster recalled Bertie's abilities and offered him the position of assistant teacher, without a salary until Bertie mastered more subjects.

It was exactly the sort of opportunity Bertie longed for, but, as always, there was a problem. Bertie was apprenticed to Southsea for four years, and he had served only two. His mother had paid forty pounds of the fifty required of apprentices. Sarah Wells collapsed in tears when her son told her of his hopes of abandoning yet another apprenticeship. How could he do this to her? Why could he not be a good boy like his brother Fred?

Bertie was no longer willing even to pretend to ambition as a draper. Not even for his mother. He turned to Joseph Wells, but found little support from his father. How could the boy consider an unsalaried job?

The family was in an uproar and nothing had been accomplished. Bertie remained trapped, and the fear grew in him that this opportunity would vanish. He had to take matters more forcefully in hand.

The chance for action arose one weekend. Upon hearing that something he'd done at the shop was so serious that Mr. Hyde himself would take charge of Bertie's punishment, Bertie fled Hyde's Southsea Drapery Emporium and began walking to Up Park. It was early Sunday morning. It was a seventeen-mile walk, but neither Bertie's courage nor his legs failed him. In his novel *Tono-Bungay*, Wells recalled walking across the huge estate's grounds, encountering the servants, all of whom were surprised to see him. Bertie walked on, steeling himself for the encounter with his mother. When he saw her he called out to her.

"My mother looked up, went very white, and put her hand to her bosom. . . ."

Sarah Wells was shocked that her son had left such a fine position as he held at Southsea. She insisted that he return immediately, but Bertie was beyond persuasion. He made several dire threats, melodramatic promises that he had no intention of keeping. Sarah finally succumbed to Bertie's pleading, and promised to think over the possibility of his returning to Midhurst Grammar School. First, though, Bertie had to go back to Southsea.

At work again Bertie made even less effort to prove a worthy employee. Bertie spent much of his time writing letters to his mother, stating and restating his unhappiness as a draper, painting a picture in words of the wonderful future that awaited him as a teacher.

Sarah gradually realized that her youngest son was not cut out for the retail trade. Now Bertie had only to persuade his father. Joseph still held his feelings about the foolishness of an unsalaried position, however, and Bertie could find no way to change his father's mind.

Then Headmaster Byatt intervened, offering to pay Bertie twenty pounds for the first year and forty pounds for the second. The salary was not luxurious, but it would enable Bertie to support himself.

Bertie had his salary and all objections evaporated.

With the salary arranged, Bertie felt impatient to leave Hyde's Southsea Drapery Emporium. He wanted to go immediately. He was eager to catch up on the schooling he'd missed during his two years at Southsea. Even Mr. Hyde's reasonable request that Bertie remain long enough to help during the large summer sale fell on unsympathetic ears. Bertie would not grant his patient employer even that small courtesy. He was too eager to be on his way.

Bertie packed his bags and prepared himself to enter another phase of his life. All hopes of his ever becoming a respectable clerk had disappeared. He was to be a teacher.

With the twenty pounds annually he would no longer need to look to his mother for help. He was on his own at the age of seventeen, no longer little Bertie but Herbert George Wells, setting out to find his world and conquer it.

THREE

THE WORLD OF EDUCATION

DISCIPLINE, ORDER, A *plan*—these were the attitudes brought by Herbert George Wells to the process of education. He made a list of proper and studious activities and posted that list on the wall of his rented room in Midhurst. He filled every moment with tasks designed to improve the quality of his thinking and the scope of his knowledge. He allowed himself no opportunity for frivolity, fun, or wasted time. He was seventeen years old and he felt that he had no time to lose. Wells's *schema,* as he called his schedule, represented his attempt to overcome his natural inclination toward an exuberant interest in everything, an inclination that could result in his becoming master of nothing.

Wells understood the importance of education. This was not simply a career; it was more than an alternative to the draper's trade. Education for Wells became his ultimate escape from the stifling world of Atlas House, from his parents' problems, from the smallness of the world in which he'd grown up. His horizons had broadened and he saw education as the tool with which he could stretch them even farther. For Herbert George Wells, everything about Midhurst marked a new beginning.

He had a companion with whom he shared this great adventure. Wells roomed with another young Midhurst teacher. Wells and his roommate often went together on long walks through the countryside, discussing ideas, comparing notes on their lessons. True to his *schema,* Wells even established a rigorous routine for these walks: one hour long over a distance of four miles.

Wells's room was above a candy store, owned by a pleasant lady who took pains to treat her tenants well. Even the meals Wells ate were part of the adventure—marvelous stews, all manners of jellies and jams, good cooking that was meant to be enjoyed. It was the first time Wells discovered true pleasure in food.

He was having the time of his life.

The only drawback during those first days at Midhurst was another encounter with religion. Sarah's lectures about a stern and vengeful God had had no effect on young Wells; he refused over and over again to join the Anglican church.

Midhurst Grammar School, however, had a rule that no teacher could hold a position unless the teacher was also a confirmed member of the Anglican church. Wells's desire to remain at Midhurst overcame his opposition to the church, and he found himself kneeling before a bishop to be confirmed.

If Sarah Wells rejoiced that her youngest son had at last seen the light and joined the faith, Wells himself was not so pleased. Throughout his life he carried a certain bitterness about the hypocrisy of his confirmation. His roommate was a devout young man, and during his time at Midhurst Wells took to taunting his roommate with mild blasphemies. As the years passed, Wells would look for and find other targets for his distrust of religion.

Once the confirmation was out of the way Wells got down to serious study. During the day he taught school, and at night he studied under Headmaster Byatt. During this season of intense study, Wells began to understand the nature of his own intelligence. He was a generalist, more at home with broad outlines of ideas and knowledge in a variety of fields than he was with intensive, specialized study of a single subject.

Wells knew the advantages of his type of mind—it allowed him to approach many different areas of learning. But he also encountered difficulties with more advanced areas of scientific study, and found some technical subjects very hard going. He came to realize "that I knew a great deal more about things in general than most of the people about me. . . ." That realization, however, "was balanced by another, that there were people in the world whose minds must be able to run and leap eagerly among these difficulties where mine wriggled and crawled painfully." Still, for all his new knowledge of his limitations, Wells studied hard throughout the year in anticipation of the May examinations.

Not all his time was spent on scientific studies. Headmaster Byatt recalled that as a young student years before, Wells had shown some talent for writing. Byatt encouraged Wells to resume his literary attempts. A few short stories flowed from the student's pen, written between tasks assigned on the *schema*. In addition, Wells began to broaden his reading habits, dipping into books on subjects more social than scientific.

One of these books was Plato's *Republic*. That great treatise, a cornerstone of political thought, exerted a profound effect on young Herbert George Wells. Plato argued that society could be changed, and that if conditions were not satisfactory, society should be changed, must be changed. Wells saw in Plato's teachings the exact opposite of Sarah's belief in the proper order of society. Wells's own memory of his unfair condemnation to the life of a draper, and the narrowness of his escape from that life, remained fresh. He responded enthusiastically to Plato's assertion that a truly good society would never put the interests of commerce before the public good. In Wells's mind the proper order of society taught by his mother began to crumble. Sarah insisted that every man was born to fill a station in life, and that most were meant to serve the few who lived at the top. Plato weakened the foundation of Wells's belief in that proper order to such an extent that a single blow could bring the entire structure to the ground.

That blow arrived in the form of a cheap paperback book Wells bought at a newsstand. The book was *Progress and Poverty* by Henry George, and it had first been published in 1879. *Progress and Poverty* held George's claim that all of society should benefit from the land, and that landlords unfairly exploited their tenants. George's solution was a tax on the landlords, a tax that would be used for the good of all tenants.

The ideas in *Progress and Poverty* seized young Wells like a fever. He could not get them out of his mind. He found himself drawn to the concept of reform, drawn as eagerly as he was to the idea of education. The idea of private property bothered him. In private property, in the concentration of wealth among the few, lay the misery of the many. Property should be owned by everyone, he thought, all working together toward a common goal.

Wells was becoming a socialist.

His mind bubbled with grand ideas for his new vision of the world. Wells would, were he in charge, end all frustration and unhappiness by creating a new order. This new order—a fair and just order of society, not simply a *proper* one—would be based upon rationalism. It would be based upon the power of thought and education rather than upon acquisition and the power of money. Like most young people, Wells thought that it would be easy to change the world. All he had to do was spread this new gospel. He spent much time taunting his poor roommate, already teased about religion, with the possibilities for a new, reorganized world.

Wells had taken on another enthusiasm.

Even as he planned the restructuring of the world, Wells

spent most of his time studying. He knew how much he had to learn, and he was also aware that the examinations in May would arrive very quickly. Winter melted away as Wells pored over his books.

When examination day arrived the long hours paid off. Wells won several awards, and earned for Headmaster Byatt, who received cash awards from the government for each student's mastery of a subject, much more than the twenty pounds Herbert had been paid for the year.

The triumph on the exams was surpassed by an unexpected honor. High scores on the examinations earned scholarships for many students. Because he had done so well on the exams Wells was offered a scholarship to the Normal School of Science in South Kensington, London. The scholarship carried a small stipend to cover Herbert's living expenses, as well as a railway ticket to London.

He accepted the scholarship immediately. Then, to his further amazement, he found that he was accepted to study "for a year in the biological course under Professor Huxley—the great Professor Huxley, whose name was in the newspapers, who was known all over the world!"

Wells could not believe his good fortune. It was as though a great treasure had been handed to him. He would be able to pursue a career in science, something that even at Midhurst had been only a vague dream. Not only that—Wells's initial studies would take place under one of the great scientists of the day, Professor Thomas Henry Huxley.

After a single year there, Wells said good-bye to Midhurst Grammar School. He'd learned a great deal, and accomplished more than he'd hoped. He would for the rest of his life recall his brief time at Midhurst as an important influence on his destiny. Eventually he would pay tribute to that year in a fine novel, *Love and Mr. Lewisham*, about a young teacher in a school similar to Midhurst.

Wells used the summer before entering Normal School to good advantage. He knew that he had fences to mend with his family, and during the recess he visited both his mother and his father.

Sarah Wells, true to her nature, was not pleased at the prospect of her son venturing to London to study science. She had no use for science; it played little part in her proper order of things. Besides, she had heard many terrible rumors about Professor Huxley. Surely little Bertie could learn nothing worthwhile from such a man. Sarah had even heard that Huxley was an atheist.

Wells was no longer "little Bertie," and he had figured out a scheme for dealing with his mother. He told her that Huxley was dean of the Normal School, which was true. He did not, however, tell her that in this case "dean" was a school title, rather than a church title, as Sarah was familiar with the word. Sarah assumed then that Huxley must be a church official, and she relaxed somewhat.

That summer Sarah was still living at Up Park, and after his visit there, Wells returned to Atlas House for a reunion with his father.

For the past three years Wells had hardly seen his father. Now, at last, they spent some time getting to know each other. Joseph lived alone in Atlas House, and the quarters were sloppy and in disarray. Young Wells did not mind. There was little business left, save the occasional purchase of some piece of cricket equipment. Joseph was growing fat, and he walked with difficulty. Yet that summer was one his son would remember clearly all his life, for it was the first time he truly felt close to one of his parents.

Joseph was pleased and proud of his son's academic accomplishments. He listened carefully as the young student explained scientific subjects. Joseph displayed to his son a mind far more interested in the workings of the universe than Wells had ever imagined. Joseph spoke of nights in his own youth, bright cloudless nights when he would lie on his back and stare up at the immensity of the universe, wondering what forces formed it, curious as to what lay beyond it.

Wells had no idea that his father, who had always seemed to him cold and distant, uninterested in anything except cricket, had always harbored such thoughts.

They went for long walks, discussing literature and philosophy. As the summer wore on, the natural hesitation between father and son disappeared. They debated every subject imaginable, becoming more like friends than parent and child. Wells, so proud of what he had learned from books about the natural world, found his store of facts thin and unimpressive when compared to Joseph's accurate and practical knowledge of nature. Joseph had been a gardener before taking up Atlas House, and on his walks with his son he would point out all manner of things—plants, animals, and insects—which Wells might otherwise have ignored.

They were never again so close, but they were never again distant. During this brief summer visit, Herbert George Wells and his father, Joseph, found themselves with a great deal in common. The older man looked back on his life and the way it had unfolded; his son looked ahead, confident but not yet certain what awaited him.

At summer's end Wells left Atlas House for the journey to London and the Normal School. He'd finally gotten to know his father, finally freed himself from any prospect of a life in commerce, finally placed himself upon a path that promised satisfaction and possible success

It was as though, at last, his life was truly beginning.

FOUR

THE WORLD OF SCIENCE

WELLS ARRIVED IN SOUTH KENSINGTON in September of 1884. He was eighteen years old and filled with eagerness to begin his new career.

Everything was so exciting. *Science!* It was the golden dream of the nineteenth century, the new art that would transform life into paradise for all. Through science, it was promised, men would become gods. There seemed, in those years, no promise science could not fulfill.

It had already fulfilled many. Beginning with Thomas Newcomen's invention of the steam engine, and James Watt's later improvements on it in the eighteenth century, science and technology had transformed English life. The steam engine took the place of human laborers at many tasks, increasing efficiency, making possible industrial production on a scale never before possible. The steam engine powered the change in England from an economy based upon agriculture to one based upon industry. Factories rather than fields became the backbone of England; workers earned their livings at machines rather than behind plows. The Industrial Revolution that swept across England in the first half of the nineteenth century was one of the most dramatic periods of change in man's history. Its effects were still being felt when Wells arrived at the Normal School.

England was desperate for science teachers, and the Normal School of Science was an institution created to help satisfy that need. The steam engine, and later electricity, had been taken from the laboratory and put to work in factories, on rail lines, in mines, and at sea. Practical applications of scientific work had made many people wealthy.

But they had also made many people miserable. While the factory owners grew wealthy, their workers were underpaid, often worked more than twelve hours a day, frequently began their careers in the factory when they were children. Other effects of applied science and technology could be seen: Cities collected hazes of industrial smog, buildings grew grimy with soot from coal-burning engines, rivers became thick with industrial wastes.

And there were not enough jobs to go around. The Industrial Revolution had beckoned people from the fields, but the factories, despite the explosive growth in their number, could not accommodate all who answered the call. Thousands were poverty-stricken, dying by the score in poorhouses, starving on the streets. These were the people who had joined the exodus to the cities in search of work, and who had not been lucky enough to find a twelve-hour-a-day job in a factory. London in 1884 was home to one-seventh of England's population. The city could boast of Europe's highest standard of living, in its West End; but it also possessed, in its slums, the poorest standard of living in Europe.

The conditions could not be ignored. Some people, such as Henry George in *Progress and Poverty* and Charles Dickens in his great novels, cried for reform. But reform was something more easily demanded than accomplished.

The social problems had, at least indirectly, been caused by science, and there were those who felt that their solutions must lie in science. Certainly young Herbert George Wells felt that this was so. He still carried with him his youthful dreams of Plato's world: a world set free from petty problems, a world of people liberated to pursue more noble dreams and aspirations. A world, thought Wells, free to immerse itself in Ideas, not in mere greed or subsistence.

But greed and subsistence were two sides of the same coin. The problems many wanted science to solve were not the problems of poverty and deprivation, but the problems of further increasing industrial production in order to better compete with other manufacturing nations. Science teachers were needed to instruct the technicians and scientists who would increase production, thus bolstering the higher standards of living while also helping to raise the lower classes from their misery.

The Normal School was only part of England's belated attempt to improve the quality of education. The school's full name was the Normal School of Science and Royal School of Mines, and its ultimate goals were as much practical as they were intellectual.

Wells's goals were different. He was intrigued with ideas for their own sake, and the scientific idea that most fascinated him was the idea of evolution, an idea that had few, if any, practical applications.

Evolution was a strong, almost blasphemous concept at that time. In many eyes it was purely blasphemous and nothing else. Controversy had surrounded the theory of evolution since the publication of Charles Darwin's *The Origin of Species* in 1859. This brilliant book, which sold out its entire first printing within hours of publication, was recognized from the moment it appeared as one of the great scientific books, a classic of research and documentation. Its argument was presented in its full title: *On the Origin of Species by Means of Natural Selection, or the Preservation of Favoured Races in the Struggle for Life.*

Darwin's argument in this book was based upon his rigorous observations of the natural world. From those observations he had learned that different species of animals were adapted to the various challenges their environments presented. If a finch, for example, was adapted to a diet of seeds, and the seed supply dramatically diminished, the population of finches would also decrease. If some finches, however, were able to eat insects, and the supply of insects was sufficient for food, those finches would thrive. Nature provided food, and those creatures most able to find and eat that food were those that would survive and pass their characteristics on to their offspring. This process of adapting to the environment and passing on those characteristics that made for the most successful adaptation was known as natural selection.

It followed from this argument that the origin of all life must have been in simple organisms, eons in the past, which themselves adapted, developed new characteristics, and passed those characteristics on to subsequent generations. All life, then, was a process of development of survival characteristics and the transmission of those characteristics to descendants.

This bold theory seemed to many to be a refutation of religion, a taunt aimed at the orthodox view of both world and life as divinely inspired, God-created. Darwin himself would not respond publicly to these charges; he was a gentle and unassertive man in many ways, who only wanted to get on with his work. His voice in public debates was taken by many colleagues, but none was so effective as Professor Thomas Henry Huxley.

Huxley, born in 1825, had made his own contributions to scientific knowledge. Among other things he had given the name Coelenterata to the phylum to which jellyfish belong. But it was as a popularizer of science, an explainer, that Huxley gained his long-lasting fame.

Unlike Darwin, Huxley was not shy. He argued forcefully and well in private and in public that evolution was the explanation of man's origin. In a much-publicized debate with a prominent Anglican bishop, Huxley attracted a great deal of attention by announcing his preference for an ancestry traced through the apes and lower orders than one traced through men of such foolish pretensions as those of the church. Huxley was a sensation, and he was as effective in the classroom as he was upon the debating stage.

Wells was seized by the theory of evolution, and he became equally obsessed with the idea of science as the great salvation of mankind. But first, he knew, the average citizen must be made aware of the promise of science. This could only happen by way of teachers, explainers like Huxley. Wells threw himself into his studies with more ferocity than he'd shown at Midhurst. He wanted to be another Huxley.

It did not take long for Wells to discover that there was more to science than ideas. Despite his intense interest and the high marks he'd earned in scientific courses at Midhurst, Wells's familiarity with basic science was less than complete. He did not possess all the primary knowledge he needed. Before arriving at the Normal School, Wells had never seen a laboratory or performed an experiment. His knowledge was all derived from books, and most of his knowledge was very general. Science, however, is based upon specifics, upon exactness. If Wells had been impressed with his father's hands-on knowledge and experience with the natural world, he soon found that such experience was even more necessary in science school.

Once again Wells found himself having to study hard to make up for lost time and fill gaps in his education.

The conditions in which he lived hardly seemed conducive to good study habits. Wells had a very small room in a house full of very small rooms. The bathroom was outside, there was no hot water, little heat. Sarah Wells had, by correspondence, found these quarters for her son, but they were hardly the sort of lodgings of which she would approve. The halls were noisy, there was much drunkenness and lewdness among the other tenants, and the landlady seemed determined to manufacture a romance between her daughter and Wells.

Still, he was in London, and he was studying under Huxley. Externals almost did not matter—the life of the mind was what Wells was after, and it was what he found.

When he was not performing experiments, Wells sat in an auditorium next to the laboratory and listened raptly to Huxley's lectures. The great professor offered exactly the introduction to advanced ideas of science that the young student desired. In Huxley's class there were no practicalities, no plans for applying the knowledge gained to business or career, no means by which Huxley's students could take their learning and transform it into a material fortune. All that mattered was the Idea, the Idea of Science.

Huxley capitivated Wells with magnificent descriptions of the nature of life. Evolution, according to Huxley, taught that the devclopment of mankind from the lower orders was random, perhaps an accident, probably temporary. But this random accident, this species created by chance, Huxley argued, possessed a mind capable of ethical, spiritual thought, a mind that could approach its problems and solve them in such a way that all men benefited. The solution to mankind's problems was possible only if men, through science, increased their dominion over the earth, over the forces of nature, re-shaped and re-created, if necessary, nature in fashions suitable to the needs and desires of men. In short, Huxley said, *man*, because of his mind, was the new master, and man, through science—a creation of that mind—could now perfect nature and eliminate the randomness of its operations. Otherwise man might be only a temporary life form, doomed to go the way of the dinosaur and the other extinct creatures of history.

Wells was entranced, hypnotized. Ideas flowed like liquid from this "yellow-faced square old man, with bright little brown eyes, lurking as it were in caves under his heavy gray eyebrows." Fifty years later Wells could still recall clearly the manner in which Huxley "lectured in a clear firm voice without hurry and without delay, turning to the blackboard behind him to sketch some diagram, and always dusting the chalk from his fingers rather fastidiously before he resumed."

So eager was Wells to soak up as much of Huxley's learning as possible that the student left his quarters early in the morning, remaining at the Normal School throughout the day, leaving in the evenings only when ordered out. Even his delight with his studies, however, could not overcome Wells's awareness of the dinginess of the surroundings in which he lived. He did not care for the lodgings his mother had found. He was uncomfortable there, one moment being forced to flirt with the landlady's daughter, the next moment finding himself the object of the landlady's own attentions. He cast about for better quarters.

This time it was Joseph Wells, not Sarah, who helped their son out of his domestic dilemma. Joseph had asked a niece in London to keep an eye on the boy. The niece shared Wells's disapproval of the house Sarah found, and quickly arranged for Wells to move to more respectable quarters, to the residence, in fact, of Joseph's sister-in-law. Aunt Mary Wells rented a room to Joseph's son, and Wells found himself settling into a comfortable house with his widowed aunt, her sister, and Mary's daughter, Isabel.

These quarters were not noticeably better than the previous ones. Aunt Mary's house was heated with coal, and everything and everyone in the house wore a permanent patina of black dust. The coal did not heat the house well. Wells often studied in his room, by the light of a single candle, with his feet wrapped in linen and stuffed in the bottom drawer of his dresser to keep them out of the cold. There were other lodgers in the house but Wells did not get to know them well. There was a one-mile walk to the campus of the Normal School.

But, for all that, Wells enjoyed the new house, and remained there throughout his years at the Normal School. His Aunt Mary liked him, and Wells got along well with her. More important, he found himself attracted to Mary's daughter, Isabel. Wells had traded one set of shabby and indifferent quarters for another, and had escaped from one landlady's daughter only to find himself captivated by another's.

During those years at the Normal School, Wells was hardly the ideal image of a romantic young man. He stood five feet five inches and weighed barely one hundred ten pounds. His clothes were threadbare, his collars yellow from many washings; he could not afford even a cheap new collar. When he examined himself in a mirror he saw a pitifully thin body, with ribs apparent under sallow skin. His body was not attractive by any means, and Wells spent a great deal of time worrying about that, for he was beginning to be interested in young women.

If Wells did not possess the good looks and easygoing manner that seemed to impress many girls, he compensated by developing a quick tongue, a talent at argument and lively conversation. He used this ability to expound on any issue that came into his mind. Wells spoke constantly, eagerly, unstoppably. On several occasions he found himself holding forth to a group of students, tossing ideas at them willy-nilly, creating a dramatic impression they would not forget. Wells might not impress girls with his clothes or his physique, but he could hypnotize them with his way with words.

Soon it became obvious that those words were directed at his cousin, Isabel. He was taken with her from the first moment they met. She was his own age, "a dark-eyed girl . . . [with] broad brows and a particularly beautiful mouth and chin and neck." Isabel worked for a photographer, and often Wells would walk her to work in the morning. From the very beginning they found in each other shared interests, similarities of spirit. Soon after he moved into Aunt Mary's house,

Wells and Isabel were sneaking away to kiss and talk of the future.

It was a future that appeared especially bright. His first year at the Normal School was a great success. Fired by the magnificence of Huxley's teaching, thrilled by his own intense interest in biology, Wells studied hard, applying his mind and learning all he could.

He was one of only three students who passed Huxley's course with first-class honors, easily winning renewal of his scholarship. Wells left London to spend the summer with, in turn, Sarah and Joseph. But he left full of hopes: He was in love—with Isabel and with the prospect of a great career in science.

FIVE

THE DREAM OF SCIENCE FADES

WELLS'S SECOND YEAR AT the Normal School started with the same sense of excitement. However, it did not take long for him to realize that the first year's successes would not be repeated. Huxley was no longer among Wells's teachers.

In later life Wells would look back on that first year as "beyond all question, the most educational year of my life." The lessons he learned were important, but his enthusiasm was as much a result of the dynamic Huxley as his own resources. Without Huxley to inspire him, Wells's schoolwork slipped quickly.

During the second year he studied physics. He discovered that he was almost totally inept at laboratory experiments. He paid little attention to the teacher, and threw together his experiments in an uncaring, haphazard way. In fact, the only distinction Wells gained in physics was constructing a piece of experimental equipment so slipshod and poorly assembled that the Normal School saved it for years and displayed it as an example of how *not* to build an experiment!

No matter how hard he tried, Wells could not master physics. The science of matter and laws of nature did not seize him as biology had. It took years for Wells to understand why. The language of physics, then as today, was mathematics, and this contributed to Wells's difficulties. In Huxley

Wells had found a teacher who couched the most complex ideas in simple, clear, and graceful language; Darwin himself was a believer in a clear, understandable style—he was all for "throwing eloquence to the dogs." Decades after his Normal School days, Wells still felt that the Huxleys and Darwins—the explainers—of physics still had not arrived.

In addition to his problems with the mathematical vocabulary of physics, the subject was not well taught at the Normal School. The teacher was ill and often distracted. Because he spent so much time struggling to learn the basics, Wells was unable with physics to make the leap to great speculative thoughts as he had been with biology. Physics was one science Wells would never master.

By the end of his second year, Wells earned only a single first-class award, and that was for a minor course in geometric drawing. He actually failed more than one course. There seemed no way for his scholarship to be renewed. He found himself putting all thoughts of Isabel from his mind while he began a desperate search for a job.

The desperation proved premature. Wells barely won his scholarship for his third and final year at the Normal School. He returned from summer vacation full of good intentions, planning to study hard, once more to make up for time lost and time wasted, to make himself into a scientist and take advantage of the great opportunity the scholarship represented.

It was not to be. The third year's primary subject was geology. While physics daunted Wells because of his inability to perform experiments, geology simply bored him. As taught at the Normal School, geology consisted of students learning the names of various minerals and rock formations, studying a few fossils, memorizing data as though they were names on a map. Wells wanted a science that asked fundamental questions, one that attempted to bring an entire body of knowledge into order. His geology courses did no such thing, and

Wells soon surrendered to his apathy. He did not consider geology, as it was taught, to be a real science, and he did not apply himself to mastering it. The classroom could no longer hold him. As he had realized earlier, he was a whiz at general subjects and broad outlines. But when asked to dig too deeply, to discipline himself to the serious study of a subject that did not captivate him, he simply turned his head and went off in search of other enchantments. In many ways he was still young Bertie Wells, the spoiled child who wanted everything his own way.

He found his new enchantments in several places.

He knew that he could talk well, that he had the talent for carrying on a long monologue without losing the interest of his audience. It was natural for him to become involved in the Normal School debating society. This society met in the basement of the school, holding their gatherings by flickering gaslight amid stored experiments and equipment.

The society's format was simple: A paper would be presented by one of its members, and then the paper would be discussed and argued over by all of the members. Any subject could be discussed except religion and politics. Wells, already discovering the delights of being at the center of controversy, managed to bring up either religion or politics—and sometimes both forbidden subjects at once—every time he spoke. Once, his arguments were so objectionable that the other members of the debating society carried him bodily from the room.

In addition to spreading his beliefs through exuberant conversation and debate, Wells began writing again. He had never completely given up the process of committing his thoughts to paper, but during his third year at the Normal School he began writing in earnest, spending time hunched with pen in hand, pushing at the task of shaping sentences and molding those sentences into paragraphs and pages.

Together with several student friends he devised and

launched a small magazine of opinion, the *Science Schools Journal*. Its first issue appeared in 1886. Its editor was Herbert George Wells.

He did not hold the position long. He was constantly being scolded by the administration of the Normal School for cutting classes, for poor performance, for any number of infractions and irresponsibilities. Although he was soon forced to give up his editorship, Wells did not stop writing pieces for the *Journal*.

His subject matter as a writer was similar to the topics he discussed with the debating society: science, politics, religion, the future. In the *Journal*, however, Wells gave his imagination even freer rein than in conversation. He spun out great visions of both the near and far future. Some of these pieces were slight and humorous, others were serious. Some satirical, others romantic. Again and again he approached his paper and took up his pen to tell stories of futures in which men had evolved to the point of pure intelligence, masters of the forces of nature.

And so even as his career as a scientist or science teacher was foundering on reefs of indifference, Wells began setting a new course for himself. He was to be a writer.

He had little choice. It was obvious even to imaginative Wells that he would never become a scientist. The third-year winter examinations did not go well for him. He earned no better than a second-class mark, barely good enough to keep him in school for the final semester. He knew that he had a better than average mind, but his grades were below average.

The final semester arrived, the season that should have seen the culmination of his dreams. But even during that semester Wells made little effort to save his career. He had been too firmly seized by the world of writing, the universe of literature. He took to cutting even more classes, spending his hours reading history or studying art, subjects far removed from geology, in which he did so poorly.

When, at the end of the semester, with examinations approaching, he tried to impose some discipline upon himself, he failed once more. He vowed that he would study hard, and for every two hours of diligent schoolwork he would reward himself with fifteen minutes of looking at more interesting books. The fifteen minutes stretched into hours, whole days spent poring over great books and magnificent collections of paintings. Literature beckoned—geology was forgotten.

The results were inevitable.

In the summer of 1887 Wells failed his final geology examination. He would receive no degree from the Normal School. He would never become a scientist.

Only after he failed did his predicament seem to make an impression on him. Wells had gotten so far on his glib tongue and eager mind, making his way on generalities and brashness, that at first he could not really believe he had failed. Surely he could talk his way out of it.

Soon, though, there was no choice but belief. Wells *had* failed.

Not long after the exams, when the reality of his situation finally broke through his false confidence, Wells began answering advertisements for teaching positions. He did not really think he would find a post. Who would hire someone who had failed his final examination? What is to become of me now? he wondered mournfully.

He could not face his parents. He loved Isabel, or thought he loved her, but he could offer her no future. All of his friends had passed their examinations, received their degrees, and were moving away to begin careers as scientists or teachers, or to pursue further study. But what could Herbert George Wells do? Despair washed over him.

He thought that he might become a writer, but there seemed little prospect of finding success at writing while staying in London. There were no jobs in London; it was, after all, the city with the worst slums in Europe—too many people had come to London in search of work. It was no place to try to learn the craft of writing, and even Wells knew that he could not begin to make a living as a writer simply by deciding to. His only hope was to find a teaching position that would pay him enough to live on while he improved as a writer.

Despite his academic failure, there were a few jobs available. They were not so glorious or high-paying as those he could have obtained if his entire record had remained at the level of his first year, but they were jobs.

A position was available at the Holt Academy, a small school far off in Wales. It was not much of a job, and it was a long distance from Isabel. But Wells knew he had no choice. He packed his bags, said farewell to Isabel, and left London and the dreams of a scientific career far behind.

SIX

A NEW CAREER CALLS

WELLS RETURNED TO TEACHING with far less enthusiasm than he felt when he first apprenticed at Midhurst Grammar School. Three eventful years had passed, after all, and during those years he had moved from adolescence into young manhood. He had seen his hopes and ambitions rise during classes with T. H. Huxley, and then felt the bitter disappointment and self-loathing that accompanied the collapse of his dreams. He had fallen in love. He had discovered an ability to debate, a talent for writing. He had learned much about the nature of his intelligence. He had not mastered his courses, but he had *learned*, learned hard lessons about real life. As he approached his job in Wales, Wells knew that now he had to get by however he could, and he knew that there was no one to blame but himself. He would not let himself fail again.

The Holt Academy was a grimy, dingy, dim school. It was not academically sound. Its classrooms were filthy, its headmaster and his wife had little interest in education, classes were unplanned and unscheduled. There was no discipline. Boarding students slept two and three to a bed.

Wells forced himself to ignore these problems. He set to work. He reminded himself that he had no choice—he needed the job. The headmaster asked little of him; Wells was left to his own devices. He tried to teach what he could, including, oddly for agnostic Wells but a part of the job, a course in Scriptures every Sunday. In his spare time he got exercise playing cricket and soccer.

And of course he wrote. That was the plan, after all, the whole reason for being in that depressing place. He was working toward a greater end, toward the goal of making his way as a writer. Letters to his friends came first, long letters, during the writing of which he became accustomed to sitting at a desk, to working with words. Many of the letters were illustrated with clever drawings, which Wells called "picshuas." Soon he began to work on short stories, working hard, serious about his career.

His industry did not last. Unhappiness overcame him. His writing output dwindled. Why bother? he wondered. Once again he was the child who would do nothing if he could not have everything his own way. He detested Holt Academy and began seeking a means of escape.

No easy escape came to hand. He had no money, no other prospects. It became clear to Wells that he was once again caught, and that freedom would only come with the passage of time. He made a plan. He would spend a year in Wales. He would save his money. He would force discipline upon himself and spend his spare time improving his writing.

He also spent time outdoors, getting exercise. He was no athlete. At Holt he found himself competing with larger boys, younger than Wells but bigger, solid farm boys accustomed to rough-and-tumble sports with few rules. In late August 1887, one of these boys fouled Wells during a football game. Wells fell to the ground. While he lay there, someone kicked him in the back.

The boys made fun of their teacher as he limped from the field. Wells ignored them. He could no longer play. He was dizzy, in great pain. He returned to his quarters, where he became sick and went to bed.

This was no simple bruise following a rough game. Before

the night was over, Wells began to pass blood. Before morning he had become delirious. A doctor was summoned.

Wells's left kidney had been crushed. The doctor confined Wells to bed. The seriousness of the injury impressed the boys in the school, and they began to develop a sort of respect for their young teacher.

For a month Wells lay in bed recovering, thinking about his future, once more uncertain as to what lay ahead.

By early October, although he was still stiff, Wells returned to work. It was too soon. He developed a cough and soon was coughing up blood. The doctor returned and it did not take long for him to determine that Wells had tuberculosis. This was a dread disease in those days before careful and constant public health measures, along with modern antibiotics, made tuberculosis a rarity. In 1887 tuberculosis was a very serious and frightening disease.

It did not matter to Wells—he needed money, he had to continue teaching.

To his football injury and the tuberculosis, Wells soon added other problems. His confidence began to falter once more. Would tomorrow ever again look as bright as it had when he first approached the Normal School? Would he throw away every opportunity and chance that came his way? What about Isabel? How could he ever hope to support a wife and family? Was he doomed, by some flaw in his own nature, to spend the rest of his life teaching uninterested youngsters in small, dirty schools such as Holt?

But he was not even to remain at Holt half a year. Sarah Wells intervened once more. Upon hearing that her son was afflicted with tuberculosis, Sarah persuaded Miss Fetherstonhaugh to allow the young teacher to recuperate in the comfort of Up Park. By early November Wells had returned to the great estate, which had harbored him so many times before.

While recuperating, Wells made many small jokes about his illnesses. In truth his condition was quite serious. Some of the health problems would plague him for the rest of his life. Fortunately, during his stay at Up Park, another resident was a young physician, Dr. William Collins. Collins refused to listen to Wells's plans for a life as an invalid. Collins insisted that Wells could make a complete recovery if he rested and took care of himself. For once Wells did the sensible thing. He took it easy, letting his body heal, relaxing, writing.

December 1887 brought to Up Park the cheeriness of the holiday season. Wells involved himself in the merriment, and the good spirits seemed to help him through the difficult transition from independent young teacher to, once again, young man dependent upon the good graces of his mother and her employer. Over Christmas Wells also visited his father, who had at last sold Atlas House and had taken up residence in a small cottage just a few miles from Up Park.

But Wells's cheerfulness did not last. Once the holidays were over he grew glum. What did he have? What lay ahead of him? He did not really want to return to the sort of teaching as practiced at Holt Academy and similar schools, but with his academic record he could not hope for a better position.

In desperation for a more secure future, he wrote twice to Dr. Collins in London, asking the physician for help in obtaining a job of any sort with someone of intellectual and social prominence. But Collins could not help Wells.

As 1888 began, Wells increased his efforts at writing. He worked at a novel considerably more ambitious than any of his short pieces. The book came quickly, pages piling up, but Wells was not satisfied with it.

At Up Park he took full advantage of the magnificent library, burying himself in novels and poetry. He began to realize that, again, he had been deluding himself. As with his dream of becoming a scientist, his dream of writing was mere wishful thinking. He had not really applied himself to the job. His scribblings were just pieces of writing, stories without commitment and involvement. Trivia.

Wells knew that he had a gift for learning and for writing. It was during his convalescence at Up Park that he also came to realize that he lacked any sort of discipline. He went too quickly for the glib line. He talked boldly and constantly, throwing away ideas without developing them. If something bored or baffled him he did not ask why, he simply turned away. A writer? He knew that he had never really worked at becoming a writer.

He finally understood that his future as a writer would depend not so much on his finding a job for a while as he wrote, but on finding some necessary employment to pay his bills while he spent the rest of his time "learning to write." Wells once more set about in search of a position.

He felt that he had to get out of Up Park. Fortunately, a friend from the Normal School, William Burton, offered to take Wells in as a guest. By early spring the arrangements were made, and in April Wells arrived in Stoke on Trent, an industrial city in west central England.

Wells came to the Burtons' home in less than good condition. As he stepped off the train his lungs hemorrhaged and he began to cough up blood. He had come to a new place but he quickly returned to the familiar isolation of the bedridden.

Burton and his wife cared for Wells, and he repaid them in the only way he could, with entertaining conversation. He was still a great talker, as Burton recalled from the days of the debating society. And still, as at the Normal School, Wells often turned his conversation into attacks on institutions and individuals. The Burtons were frequently shocked by Wells's boldness and lack of courtesy, but they cared for him and indulged his infractions. He began to grow well once more.

Wells also began to write more seriously than ever before. It was clear to him that writing was not a vocation to be pursued on a whim, but a craft that calls for inflexible discipline and endless hours of hard work. There is no other way. Now came the hardest work Wells had ever undertaken.

The Burtons lived in Staffordshire, a great industrial county crowded with smoking chimneys and blazing furnaces. It was an alien region for Wells and he wandered through it fascinated, as though touring another world. Perhaps this was his subject matter, he thought, this meeting of modern industry and the countryside. He began planning an ambitious work about the region, along with several less ambitious short stories.

He was writing with dedication now, serious at last, seeking to master his craft. Many pieces were begun and left unfinished, but he learned something from each of them. He worked on a variety of things while staying with the Burtons. Among his projects was a romance for the *Science Schools Journal,* the magazine he'd helped found. The romance was in three installments, with a fourth promised before Wells broke off. He realized that he had the foundation of a fine story, but he also knew that he did not possess the ability to complete it. That would come with time. The unfinished story was called *Chronic Argonauts,* and it dealt with voyagers through time. Wells knew that he would return to it one day.

Summer arrived, and with the coming of pleasant weather Wells's health returned. He felt stronger each morning, able to do more. His irrepressible energy was returning and with it came the urge to try once more to find fortune in London. For nearly a year he had been confined to bed, in Wales, at Up Park, at the Burtons', and he thought now that it was high time for his convalescence to end. He was a man now, and he saw that if he wanted to succeed he had to work, to pursue success with all his strength and talent. Success would not come to him simply because he thought he deserved it.

Late in his life he recalled a summer afternoon during his stay with the Burtons. Wells had gone for a long walk, and stopped in a gentle glade, a peaceful and idyllic spot in the midst of the factories. Sitting there in the warm sun, healthy at last, Wells found himself inspired. He spoke aloud. " 'I have been dying for nearly two-thirds of a year, and I have died enough.' "

He walked rapidly to the Burtons' home. He was filled with a great excitement. His spirit soared above the smoke-stacks, high in the sky

To his hosts' surprise—and, Wells guessed, their relief—he announced that he was returning to London in two weeks. He had some money—five pounds contributed by his mother. It was not much, but that five pounds would get him started once more.

As he departed the Burtons' Wells knew that he had more than just five pounds. He had his confidence back, and he had a clear vision of the goal he would pursue. That was more than fortune enough for the launching of a career.

SEVEN

A FUMBLING START

WELLS MAY HAVE BEEN ready to take on London, but the city was not yet prepared to reward his confidence. Many people, he later reflected, have more than enough confidence, and many people also have talent to accompany their confidence, but those two qualities alone do not ensure success.

Few jobs were available. Wells's five pounds did not last long, no matter how carefully he marshaled his funds. He forced himself to eat little, despite his need for solid, regular meals in order to preserve his health. He wrote to a few friends requesting aid, but they could do little to help him. Soon his money had dwindled so low that he could not afford even postcards on which to write for help.

Finally an evening arrived when he took inventory of his worldly possessions and found himself bankrupt. His clothes were worn, his collars yellow with age, his socks thin and holey. The contents of his pockets, he saw, were equally pitiful—a small piece of India rubber, a pocketknife, and a halfpenny. That halfpenny was not even enough to purchase a meal of the poorest quality. Wells lay down on his bed that evening without hope, his confidence in as much disrepair as his clothing. Had he failed again?

The next morning he noticed something strange about the halfpenny. It was blackened and old, and upon closer inspection he saw that it was not a halfpenny at all, but a shilling. A shilling! Not a fortune, but enough to stave off disaster for a while.

The first thing he did was buy a hearty, nourishing breakfast. Never had food tasted so wonderful.

Small wonders of other sorts came his way during the next few days. He had written to a Normal School friend, A. V. Jennings, and told him of his plight. There was no despair in Wells's message—it was a simple drawing, a "picshua" showing Wells with pen in hand studying a sign that announced jobs for men willing to wear advertising signs. Wells's note was brief; it told Jennings that this time he was serious about making a success in London, even if he had to resort to common labor while he worked at it.

Jennings got the message. He recalled Wells's abilities as an artist. He hired Wells to prepare a series of biological wall diagrams that Jennings would use in his position as a teacher of biology.

Wells took to the new work eagerly. His enthusiasm was not simply a result of the income, which was small. This was an opportunity to work once more, however peripherally, in education. The job also left Wells time to pursue other income from small tutoring tasks, as well as writing. He was actually paid for some minor pieces of journalism, receiving small fees for writing questions and answers about science for newspapers. Things were looking up once again.

As soon as he began to receive money from Jennings, Wells looked for new lodgings. He was sick of the miserable little room he was staying in. He wrote to his cousin, Isabel. He had never forgotten her.

Aunt Mary and Isabel had moved since Wells last stayed with them. Now they lived in an attractive and comfortable house near Regents Park. Aunt Mary's fondness for Wells remained, and she quickly offered him a room. Wells moved in.

Isabel was bringing in a fair income as a photograph re-toucher. Wells realized that he and his cousin had both grown up during their separation. For all the changes, Isabel remained as attractive as when they first met. Soon she and Wells were keeping constant company again, going for long walks, stealing furtive kisses. Aunt Mary assumed that Wells and Isabel were to marry, and she treated him as though he were her daughter's fiancé. Wells offered few objections, although he claimed not to believe in engagement. Nevertheless, he was fond of Isabel and found her as sweet and innocent as a dream. Himself he thought of as neither sweet nor innocent. He had seen too much, he wanted too much from life. He would not be satisfied with simple domesticity. Wells knew that when he and Isabel set out on their long walks, their thoughts and emotions were far apart.

The drawings for Jennings went well. Meanwhile, Wells continued to earn additional money from various other undertakings. At the same time he did not give up his search for more substantial employment, preferably a job in teaching. Wells remained full of ideas about education, proper education. He longed for the opportunity to put some of those ideas to work.

By Christmas 1888 he had found a new teaching position. He was to teach at the Henley House School in Kilburn. It was not a very successful school, at least financially. Wells's earnings remained low. But it was a teaching position, it was close enough that he could live with Aunt Mary and Isabel, and it left him free to write. He also went back to school, determined to finish his degree, working hard for honors in the study of zoology and, of all things, the geology he disliked.

His duties at Henley House School were pleasant. He enjoyed the atmosphere, was provided with fine meals, and was given a free hand to teach as he thought best. Wells thought that the best way to teach science was without practical examples or experiments, and his courses consisted of passing his enthusiasm on to his students without using examples at all.

His diligent study paid off. On his mid-year exams he scored very well, winning several prizes and earning a small raise from his employer. He continued to pursue his degree, putting his writing aside for the time being.

In the summer of 1890 he left Henley House School for another teaching job, this one as a biology instructor with the University Correspondence College. It was not much of a position, consisting primarily of tutoring students in the proper answers to the most commonly asked questions on college biology exams. Wells's position required that he concern himself not with the speculative aspects of biology, which so intrigued him, but only with cramming his students' heads full of information so that they might earn high grades on their examinations.

It was not the sort of education he preferred, but the job paid a higher salary than he'd earned before. When Wells passed his final exams and was granted a degree—with first-class honors in zoology—his salary was increased. The extra money made him able to consider marriage. He was well aware that he and Isabel did not have a great deal in common, but Wells found himself more and more thinking of marriage to Isabel as the natural consequence of their relationship. They had been brought together by chance, but they had found themselves to be friends, and each of them felt in love with the other. Wells and Isabel sought to be everything to each other, to fulfill their ideals of love and marriage.

Wells did not completely neglect his writing. During a brief relapse into illness he returned to Up Park for a month. As he recuperated he wrote an article called "The Rediscovery of the Unique," which was his most ambitious piece of writing yet. It dealt with Wells's theories and beliefs about the mysteries, the *uniqueness*, of life. It marked a return to his love of scientific speculation, of using science as a philosophy, rather than as a mere practical tool for naming things and fashioning laws. When he finished the article he mailed it off to *Fortnightly Review,* an important journal.

To Wells's astonishment the piece was accepted, and Wells's dream of a writing career was once again kindled. He quickly sat down and wrote another piece, equally ambitious, called "The Universe Rigid." He sent the new piece also to *Fortnightly Review.*

The editors were delighted that the author of "The Rediscovery of the Unique" had submitted another article. Its pages were sent immediately to the printers. Only when the printed sheets were returned was the new piece closely examined by the editors. They discovered, to their horror, that "The Universe Rigid" made absolutely no sense. Frank Harris, the senior editor, immediately sent for Wells.

Wells was nervous about the meeting. Harris was a famous man, an important editor and writer. It was important to Wells that he make a good impression, and he went to great pains to dress formally, wearing an old silk hat, which he wetted with a sponge in order to improve its shabby appearance. He hurried to Harris's office.

He was kept waiting for half an hour. Finally he was summoned to meet the important editor. Wells's nerves were completely raveled, he could barely speak. He would never forget the interview with Harris, and would recall their conversation in his autobiography.

Wells stared at Harris and thought that he had never met so fierce and intimidating a figure.

"And it was *you* this 'Universe R-R-Rigid'!" Harris shouted at the frightened young author.

Wells sat down opposite Harris. He said nothing. He placed his silk hat on the table and then noticed that the wetting, which had been intended to improve the hat's appearance, had actually destroyed what few good features it had. The hat was a mess. Harris stared at it, then back at Wells.

"You sent me this 'Universe Gur-R-R-Rigid'?" Harris growled again.

Wells said nothing.

Harris picked up the article, waved the pages at Wells. "Dear Gahd! I can't understand six words of it. What do you *mean* by it? For Gahd's sake tell me what it is all *about*. What's the sense of it? What are you trying to *say*?"

"Well, you see—" Wells began.

"I don't see! That's just what I don't do."

"The idea—" Wells began again. He fumbled for an explanation. The article was about space and time. He tried to explain.

"I can't use it," said Harris, and sent Wells away.

Wells had met his first editor.

1891 brought more successes than defeats to Wells. "The Universe Rigid" may have been rejected, but "The Rediscovery of the Unique" caught the eye of many influential readers. Wells's teaching income rose steadily. He rented a small house.

He and Isabel moved closer to marriage, and on October 31, 1891, they were wed. Wells knew that he and his cousin were in many ways dissimilar—she had no interest in his speculations, and he was less than excited by simple domestic details—but they had "courted" for so long the marriage became inevitable. He and Isabel, along with Aunt Mary, settled into the house.

It was soon obvious that Wells's marriage was not a happy one. The differences between Wells and Isabel, which while they were courting he had assumed could be overcome, grew more serious. Their temperaments did not match, their physical needs were far apart. Within a few months of his marriage Wells began casting his eyes toward other young women, women who might more clearly approach him in nature. He began to think of the ideal woman, a match in physical and emotional desire and intellectual adventurousness.

And he continued to write. The fiasco of "The Universe Rigid" had not smashed his hopes. He found other small writing jobs and gradually began to undertake larger assignments. In 1892 he wrote his first real books, collaborating with Richard Gregory, another classmate from the Normal School, on *Textbook of Biology* and *Honours Physiography,* both of which were published in 1893. These were small books, booklets really, which were little more than printed versions of the cram lectures Wells gave to students. But they were books nonetheless, real writing, and Wells was on his way.

EIGHT

A WRITER OF PROMISE

IF WELLS'S CAREER WAS finally beginning to take shape, his mother's was nearing its end. Sarah was growing old, had lost her hearing, performed her duties at Up Park less and less ably. Miss Fetherstonhaugh grew increasingly dissatisfied with Sarah's work. Up Park would no longer be a welcome harbor for Wells, Joseph, or Wells's brothers, Fred and Frank.

Soon it ceased to be any sort of harbor at all.

On February 16, 1893, Miss Fetherstonhaugh discharged Sarah Wells. After a brief stay with Wells and Isabel, Sarah returned to Joseph, sharing a house with him for the first time in years. Sarah was miserable, convinced that the universe had turned against her. Joseph continued to attend cricket matches, drinking heavily. There was little money.

Wells took to sending funds to help support his parents, although his own income was hardly lavish. He worked himself hard, teaching, writing, tutoring. He was worried about his mother and how he could support her; he was unhappy with his wife and uncertain how long he could continue to live with her. And soon there was another woman for him to worry about.

Her name was Amy Catherine Robbins, and she had been one of his students for several months. He was attracted to her immediately, his interest captured not only by her beauty, her "very delicate features," but also by their shared interests. Wells grew convinced that Amy Catherine Robbins was the woman he *wanted* to marry and share his life with.

The early months of 1893 brought great strain. There were so many things on Wells's mind. Too many. He buried himself in his work, stealing time occasionally to write a flirtatious letter to Amy Robbins, then returning to his work, trying to put her from his mind.

He had no intention of being unfair or cruel to Isabel. He had known and cared for her too long for that. But it became clear to him, as their marriage passed through its eighth and ninth months, that he had married too hurriedly. They were both still so young. Neither had really loved anyone else. He did not know what to do. He could not imagine leaving Isabel, but he could not imagine spending the rest of his life with her either.

The pressure of all the different worries proved too much for him. On May 17, 1893, Wells's lungs failed again. He hemorrhaged, coughed up blood, was immediately confined to bed.

As before, he used convalescence as a period of contemplation and reflection. He planned his future. He would not teach again. His health would not support that career. He made the decision to support himself and his dependents through writing.

And the first person he told of his decision was his former student, Amy Catherine Robbins.

His mind made up, his future chosen, Wells applied himself to the business of getting well. When he was able to travel he took Isabel and her mother to the coast for a brief vacation.

Having made his decision to make a living solely by his pen, Wells still needed a means of increasing his income from writing. He lay on the beach, warming himself in the sun, reading and thinking. As he relaxed there the answer came to him.

He was reading a popular novel, *When a Man's Single*, by J. M. Barrie, author of *Peter Pan*. At one point in the novel a character gives a lecture on the secret of successful free-lance writing. The path to success, the character stated, was not through the composition of long, learned, philosophical articles. The way to make money writing was to write bright and witty pieces about commonplace subjects, topics everyone was interested in. If a writer saw a man repairing a pipe, he should write an article about it. If a writer has business with a merchant selling flower pots, he should write articles about the business, about the flower pots themselves, and another about flowers! The subjects of articles are all around young writers, Barrie said, they simply had to open their eyes and see them.

Wells felt as though his own eyes had been opened. He saw again that he had wasted time chasing generalities. "The Universe Rigid" indeed! No wonder that piece had been rejected. It made no sense, it had nothing to do with real life. He thought of the mistakes he had made—"the more I was rejected the higher my shots had flown." A rejection of a difficult piece led Wells to write another difficult piece.

Now, he knew the secret.

He put his new knowledge to work immediately. Since he'd made his discovery while staying at the beach, what could be more natural than an article called "On Staying at the Seaside"? He wrote the article immediately and mailed it to an important popular magazine called *Pall Mall Gazette*.

The article was purchased the day it arrived.

By the time the first article was bought Wells was busy with another one. The second article sold just as quickly. He went through his files of discarded pieces, and each time he came across something that showed promise he rewrote it, sent it out, and received an acceptance.

In less than three months Wells's income from writing exceeded the highest salary he'd ever earned as a teacher. He and Isabel moved to a more comfortable house. Editors began to request his work by name. He had enough money to help Sarah and Joseph.

Success did not free his mind of thoughts of Amy Robbins. Now that he was successful he wanted to share his happiness with someone other than Isabel. He could not bring himself to leave her, though. He stayed at home and wrote.

Shortly before Christmas 1893, Wells and Isabel went for a visit at the home of Amy Robbins and her mother. If Isabel had no idea of her husband's love for Amy before the visit, it all became clear soon enough. When they returned to London she issued an ultimatum.

Isabel told Wells that he must choose between their marriage and Amy Catherine Robbins. She would not tolerate the situation continuing as it was.

It was not easy for Wells. He felt guilty and depressed. But he had to do what was right for him. He could not remain with Isabel, to do so would only succeed in ruining her life along with his own.

He moved out.

Early in January 1894 Wells and Amy Robbins moved into lodgings together. The scandal created by this among their relatives threatened to destroy their life together before it was well begun. Many decades remained before couples could live together without benefit of marriage and not cause dismay to society.

But Wells and Amy knew that they belonged together. They could not wait for Wells's divorce. They were in love.

In many ways Amy Catherine Robbins was the ideal woman for Herbert George Wells. She was devoted to Wells, always placing his interests before her own. She cared for him, bore his children, supported his ego and confidence as he undertook ever more difficult and challenging writing projects. She indulged his flaws, looked the other way when his eyes wandered toward other women. Wells loved her dearly, and she loved him. They were married in 1895, and the scandal over their elopement gradually faded as it became obvious that theirs was a very happy union.

They remained together until Amy's death in 1927. Their bold and reckless act of passion united them early in 1894, when Wells was twenty-eight years old and on the edge of his first truly great success.

NINE

THE TIME MACHINE

WHEN WELLS AND AMY first moved in together they knew that there was a struggle ahead. Wells's writing was in demand but he was not yet an established name. Their first landlady strongly disapproved of their living together, and she became such an annoyance that the young couple moved.

In their new quarters they established a comfortable happy rhythm. After breakfast Wells worked hard on new articles. Amy copied articles already completed, preparing them for submission. She was also studying for her own degree in biology. Their mornings passed quickly, filled with happiness and rewarding work.

After lunch they would go for a walk together, searching for topics for new articles. True to the decision he'd made at the beach, Wells found article ideas everywhere. If he and Amy played chess, he wrote and sold an article about chess. If they toured a museum, the museum became the subject of an article.

They were deliriously happy, playful together, young people out to conquer the world. They teased and kidded each other constantly. Amy called him Bertie, and he gave her a nickname that lingered for the rest of her life. He called her Jane.

As Wells's success increased he began to vary the type of

work he did. He knew that the cheerful, trivial articles he wrote could not remain satisfying forever. They were a sort of apprenticeship, much as the time he spent in Midhurst Grammar School had been an apprenticeship in education. Just as he had moved on to more challenging teaching positions, now he was ready to move on to more challenging pieces of writing.

He had learned an important lesson, though. No more articles of pretension and murkiness, no more "Universe Rigids." As he expanded his abilities and craft, Wells began writing short stories. These met with the same success as his articles, and he was soon summoned to the office of the *Pall Mall Budget,* companion magazine to the *Gazette.*

This meeting was no disaster, as the meeting with Frank Harris had been. (And that turned out well enough after all—once Wells learned how to write successful short pieces, Harris published many articles by Wells.) The editor of the *Budget* had a proposition for Wells.

The *Budget* appeared weekly. Would Wells be interested in writing frequent short stories dealing with scientific subjects?

It was exactly the sort of work Wells desired.

He set eagerly to work, producing story after story, each turning on an unusual scientific fact or development. The stories were popular with the *Budget*'s audience, and soon Wells moved to more prestigious markets, his stories appearing in magazines such as the *Strand,* in which Arthur Conan Doyle's Sherlock Holmes had become famous.

The market for short pieces, strong and growing when Wells first began to sell, soon went through one of its periodic retreats. Some magazines told Wells they were overstocked with his work. Others went out of business. The outlets for his writing—and the sources of his income—were shrinking. He had been approached to have a book published, *Select Conversations with an Uncle,* a collection of his better magazine pieces, but it was printed in a small edition and did not bring in much income.

To add to the problems he faced, Jane was unhappy. She never wavered in her love of Wells or her support for his work, but she was under tremendous emotional pressure, from her mother, from their landladies, from acquaintances who did not approve of their relationship. They were, after all, living in sin, or so it was seen, and Jane found herself looked upon as a woman of low morals. Wells's divorce would not be final until early 1895. Could the pressures be withstood that long?

Always before when faced with strain, Wells had run away—to Up Park or to a library or to the arms of Jane. He resolved that he would not run away now.

He knew that with the shrinking of his markets he had to make a name for himself as a serious writer, a writer of substance, or he would fade as quickly as his brief pieces on chess or the seaside. Did he have anything major he could complete? His intention was supported by a lucrative offer from a major magazine for a long work, accompanied by a commitment from a book publisher to bring the work out in permanent form once serialization was complete.

He remembered the story about time travelers he'd begun for the *Science Schools Journal*. In fact, that story in the *Journal* had caught the interest of the magazine and inspired their offer.

Wells took Jane and her mother to the country for a few months while he worked on the piece.

It was his first work of real ambition, his first important work. He feared that if he failed his career would never again have the promise it now held. He did not intend to fail, and this time he held his discipline firmly in support of his intention.

He never forgot the writing of that story. Jane's mother

was sick. Jane had gone to bed. Wells sat at his desk faced with one of the most challenging portions of the narrative.

"It was a very warm blue August night and the window was wide open," he recalled years later. "Moths were fluttering in ever and again. . . . Outside in the summer night a voice went on and on. . . ." The voice belonged to Wells's landlady, and she was complaining loudly of Wells's relationship with Jane. Let her complain, Wells thought. He knew she would never confront him directly.

"It went on and on. I wrote on grimly to that accompaniment. I wrote her out and she made her last comment with the front door well and truly slammed. I finished my chapter before I shut the window and turned down and blew out the lamp.

"And somehow amidst the gathering disturbance of those days *The Time Machine* got itself finished."

The Time Machine. Written under very trying circumstances by an author still young and not fully established, with an unhappy woman living with him, the guilt over leaving Isabel still heavy within him, aware of the many failures in his past, uncertain how many more failures he could stand.

But *The Time Machine* was no failure. It was recognized as a classic from the day it appeared. It is one of the most famous stories in the English language, and it is arguably the most famous science fiction story ever written. Wells had resolved to do his best, and he succeeded in every possible way.

Wells told the moving story of the Time Traveller who visited the far, far future, and discovered the decline of mankind, its separation into two races, the gentle Eloi, the brutal Morlocks. A glimpse of the end of the world, a love story, a speculation on the nature of life in the far future, and at the same time a reflection on the nature of life in the 1890s, a story of evolution, of the difference between classes, the waste of the struggle between them, the tragedy of their lack of concern for each other.

Near the end of the book the Time Traveller voyages beyond the era of the Eloi and Morlocks; he takes his time machine to the very end of time, to the final gasp of life on earth. It was a passage on which Wells lavished his finest, most chilling prose:

"The sky was no longer blue. North-eastward it was inky black, and out of the blackness shone brightly and steadily the pale white stars. Overhead it was a deep Indian red and starless, and south-eastward it grew brighter to a glowing scarlet where, cut by the horizon, lay the huge hull of the sun, red and motionless. . . .

"The sea stretched away to the south-west, to rise into a sharp bright horizon against the wan sky. There were no breakers and no waves. . . . Only a slight oily swell rose and fell like gentle breathing, and showed that the eternal sea was still moving and living. . . .

"Far away up the desolate slope I heard a harsh scream, and saw a thing like a huge white butterfly go slanting and fluttering up into the sky and, circling, disappear over some low hillocks beyond. . . . I saw that, quite near, what I had taken to be a reddish mass of rock was moving slowly towards me. Then I saw the thing was really a monstrous crab-like creature. Can you imagine a crab as large as yonder table, with its many legs moving slowly and uncertainly, its big claws swaying, its long antennae, like carters' whips, and its stalked eyes gleaming at you on either side of its metallic front?

"I cannot convey the sense of abominable desolation that hung over the world."

The Time Traveller doubted his ability to convey his perceptions, but there was no doubt of Wells's ability. The magazine that requested the story was delighted. Wells received one hundred pounds for the serial, and another fifty pounds plus a generous royalty rate from the prestigious publisher Heinemann for the book version. (At that time, one hundred fifty pounds was approximately equivalent to a thousand dollars.)

Wells's great success had begun!

The public response to *The Time Machine* was excellent. The story grabbed readers with its first words, and held onto them through its final page. "It grips the imagination as it is only gripped by a genuinely imaginative work," wrote one reviewer. Another called the book "brilliant."

The originality of Wells's vision of the future, along with the adventurous and romantic story, delighted and intrigued readers. The depth of Wells's thinking could be found in the story, and one of the reasons for its success was that his thinking had grown more complex since he first attempted a tale of time travel. Wells no longer was convinced that science had the answers to all questions. He was thinking more deeply about the relationship between science and society, science and ethics, science and the future. Some of this could be seen in *The Time Machine*.

Editors responded to Wells's success by requesting more stories. Wells set out to produce them.

His divorce became final in January 1895, and he married Jane. He wrote *The Wonderful Visit,* a funny little novel about an angel's visit to earth. The collection of his magazine pieces was published. A collection of short stories, *The Stolen Bacillus, and Other Incidents,* appeared in November 1895.

His income for the year totaled £792, all of it earned through writing. He used a portion of his money to secure a better home for Joseph and Sarah. For himself and Jane, Wells rented a little house in the country.

The house was pleasant. Wells enjoyed living in the country. His first books were selling well and he knew that his income would continue to rise. It occurred to him that he might become wealthy from his writing. It was an amusing thought, coming less than two years after worries as to whether he could even subsist by means of his pen.

Wells looked back. He was nearly thirty years old. So many of his dreams had turned to dust. The career in science, the career as a teacher, his first marriage.

But taking the place of those dreams was a new reality. He had made his mark. He was a writer and he was going to be an important one. It would no longer do to look back, at least not too often. What mattered was the work that lay ahead, the work that was his real dream. He was no longer little Bertie Wells, no longer even Herbert George Wells the promising young journalist. He had made his name and it was neither of those.

He was H. G. Wells, and he was ready to get to work.

TEN

SCIENTIFIC ROMANCES

IN ORDER TO BRING some life to his writing career, Wells had learned to look around him for story ideas. Now, with a successful novel behind him, he made it a practice to look not only at the world in which he lived, but also at the world that lay ahead, the world of the future.

The Time Machine won an enthusiastic reception, as had Wells's short stories of science and scientists. The reading public was ready for books and stories dealing with the wonders and perils of science, and Wells gained his first great fame by successfully fusing the scientific world with the literary.

Other writers had written of the far future, of other worlds. Fantasy has been a popular form of literature since the earliest civilizations. Literature is filled with stories of strange beasts, magical lands, voyages to worlds distant from our own.

Earlier in the nineteenth century a young woman named Mary Shelley created a stir with a different kind of fantasy. She wrote a novel called *Frankenstein*, and in it told a horrifying and gripping story that probed deeply into questions concerning the responsibilities of the scientist and the dangers that might lie in unchecked scientific progress.

In the decades just preceding Wells's rise to fame, one

of the most successful novelists in the world was a Frenchman who specialized in adventurous stories about fantastic inventions, amazing journeys, and the impact of science upon the world. His name was Jules Verne.

Jules Verne and H. G. Wells would come to be known as the fathers of science fiction. Two more dissimilar parents would be hard to imagine. Verne's interest in science was deep, but it was a practical interest, the interest of a man curious about how things worked, about how scientific advances could be applied to society. Verne went to great pains to use science accurately in his stories.

Jules Verne was also more deeply convinced than Wells of the fundamental goodness of scientific progress for the human race. Born in 1828, Verne had seen the triumphs of the Industrial Revolution begin to lift people out of poverty and ignorance. Perhaps those triumphs made him more willing to side with unbridled scientific progress than Wells was. In Verne's works readers encounter the hopes and beliefs that Wells abandoned—science as benefactor, science as bright light for the future of the world, science as humanity's golden promise.

As Verne grew older his attitudes toward science began to change. He did not ignore the fact that the Industrial Revolution, and the science upon whose shoulders the revolution rode, had not brought universal prosperity. Many of Verne's later books are more pessimistic in outlook than his early exuberant adventures.

With H. G. Wells, bleakness was a characteristic from the beginning of his success with *The Time Machine*. While *The Time Machine* is an adventure story, it is also very much the story of the world running down, approaching its end. "A horror of this great darkness came on me," said the Time Traveller as he stood on the beach at the end of time. *The Time Machine* is a story that reminds its readers that no matter what heights mankind obtains, it is only a small distance when measured against the awesome, unfeeling, overwhelming immensity of the cosmos.

The underlying pessimism of the stories did not harm Wells's popularity. For one thing, that grim vision was only one aspect of Wells's work, an aspect that could be overlooked by those readers who chose to do so. *The Time Machine* and the stories and novels that followed are serious speculations, but they are also crackling good adventure stories. Few writers have equaled H. G. Wells at setting a scene, creating fascinating characters, and placing those scenes and characters in the midst of a dramatic plot.

And the near hopelessness in Wells's stories was an attraction in itself. The late 1890s brought the end of a transitional and dramatic century. It was a century that opened in candlelight and closed with electric lights chasing away the darkness; a century that began on horseback and rode to its close in automobiles; a century that began with goods produced by hand and closed with great factories producing goods in vast numbers. It was the century in which science became the pacesetter for civilization.

The last decade of the nineteenth century saw the long reign of Queen Victoria—Sarah Wells's ideal—come to a close. With the passing of Victoria (she died in 1901), England began to question the properness of the old order, began to emerge from the stuffy, solemn patterns of life which had dominated the century.

The calendar itself played a part in the appeal of bleakness. Endings of centuries exert fascinating effects on people. The closing years of a century often mingle gay abandon with despair. It is a time when many are seized by the conviction that not only the end of the century but also the end of the world is close at hand. Predictions of doom accompany the end of every century, and there will doubtless be such predictions as our twentieth century closes a few years from now.

Social attitudes and concerns are, of course, reflected in

works of art and literature, and works created at century's end reflect the mood of their times. The despair and "sophistication" that marked the close of the nineteenth century in its art has been given a name—*fin de siècle*, a French phrase meaning literally "end of century," but which has come to describe the atmosphere of the late nineteenth century.

Wells's scientific romances were *fin de siècle* works in many ways. *The Time Machine* paints a portrait of the end of the world, the far distant future when all hope is lost, when even the planets have ceased motion. In subsequent books Wells would probe more deeply into the end of civilizations —our own and those on other worlds. He would examine the effects of absolute power on scientists, he would look at battles between weak earthlings and strong invaders from other planets.

To each of these stories Wells brought his scientific training and philosophical disposition. Wells was one of the first writers to perceive that change, whether caused by science or social upheaval, was becoming the outstanding feature of modern life. And the importance of change would become even more apparent as England moved farther from the world of proper order, and deeper into the modern age.

Wells was fortunate in that his private concerns struck a sympathetic public chord. His earnings were impressive, and Wells and Jane were able to improve their standard of living. Wells enjoyed his country home and found the area around Woking, where the house was located, conducive to relaxation, reflection, and work. He and Jane became enthusiastic cyclists, pedaling their bicycles throughout the countryside, paying calls on their neighbors, many of whom did not know quite what to make of this brash young writer.

As always, Wells put his experiences into his work. Out of his bicycling experiences he cast a novel, *The Wheels of Chance*. It was a light and entertaining story of a young man employed in a drapery emporium who goes on a bicycling vacation in search of escape from his humdrum life. During the holiday he encounters a young woman who is equally eager to improve her lot in life, but who is doing so through hard work, through action rather than daydreams.

The Wheels of Chance is a pleasant, whimsical story. Between the lines of its whimsy, though, it reveals many of the preoccupations that would inform Wells's work for the rest of his life. Ideas about social rank and ambition, *the proper order of society,* the changing nature of the world—even in slight works Wells's concerns are clear. Of particular interest in *The Wheels of Chance* is Wells's portrayal of a modern woman. It is the woman, in this book, who is decisive and assertive, a break with the traditional nineteenth-century portrait of women.

Wells continued to churn out short stories. Some months saw as many as one H. G. Wells story appear each week. The short stories varied widely in mood and tone, in the nature of the ideas they contained, in plot. Many of them turned on scientific happenings, as before, but now there was Wells's underlying skepticism, his doubts about the ultimate fate of humanity, adding a new element to his scientific tales.

The scientific novel Wells wrote to follow *The Time Machine* is at the same time his grimmest, most bleak story and the best of his many novels of science. It was called *The Island of Doctor Moreau.*

It is the story of Edward Prendick, sole survivor of a shipwreck in the Pacific, who is drifting to what he assumes will be his own slow death when he is rescued and taken to a strange island.

Through swift pacing and engaging narration Wells makes the reader curious, as curious as Prendick, to know what is happening on the island. On the island is a biological station where experiments are performed. The laboratory's director is Doctor Moreau, whom Prendick recalls from London as the perpetrator of incredible biological horrors. Moreau is a vivisectionist.

Vivisection. A controversial question in the nineteenth

century, hardly less controversial today, vivisection is the dissection of living animals for scientific knowledge.

Moreau, Prendick discovers, has been experimenting on the animal life of the island, using his scientific skills to create strange misshapen creatures who must bend themselves to Moreau's Law. The *Law* is Moreau's attempt to impose civilization upon the "Beast People" he has created.

As horrifying as the descriptions of the Beast People, as horrifying as the experiments themselves, is the recitation by these altered animals of the Law by which they live:

"Not to go on all-Fours; *that* is the Law. Are we not men?

"Not to eat Flesh or Fish; *that* is the Law. Are we not men?

"Not to claw the Bark of Trees; *that* is the Law. Are we not men?"

On and on it goes, told in eerie half-human voices, Moreau's litany, a mad parody of the codes of civilization.

In *The Island of Doctor Moreau* Wells achieved a stunning success, marrying his personal and philosophical concerns perfectly to his narrative. The story never flags, its tension and suspense never ease up, yet neither does Wells allow his points to become lost in his plot. The book is frightening in the story it tells, and equally frightening in what it reveals about ourselves.

Before its publication in 1896, the book had spent some time on Wells's shelf. Its subject matter was considered too bold for readers, and indeed when it was published *The Island of Doctor Moreau* created a storm of controversy. Virtually all of the reviews were negative. "Gruesome," "disgusting," "horrible," "ghastly"—these were just some of the descriptions applied to Wells's second novel-length scientific romance.

The reviews did not bother Wells. He delighted in creating controversy. In his own way he was putting on paper the same sorts of shocking statements that had prompted his ejection from debating society meetings years before.

No one could deter him now. Wells was a successful writer, eager to solidify his reputation. No sooner had he wrapped up *The Island of Doctor Moreau* than he returned to one of its main themes, the responsibility of the scientist, in a new novel, *The Invisible Man*.

Wells applied all of his skills to the creation of a fast-paced plot, which was becoming his storytelling trademark, and in the telling of his story made something more of it than just a simple story. Wells was already pushing at the boundaries of the scientific romance, working hard to transform adventure tales into novels of ideas.

After an engaging opening section in which a mysterious and bandaged stranger appears in a small town on a snowy night, Wells presents the suspicions of the townspeople, creating memorable characters even when they only appear for a paragraph or two.

And then Wells reveals his stranger's secret:

". . . He removed his spectacles and everyone in the bar gasped. He took off his hat, and with a violent gesture tore at his whiskers and bandages. For a moment they resisted him. A flash of horrible anticipation passed through the bar. 'Oh, my Gard!' said some one. Then they came off.

"It was worse than anything. Mrs. Hall, standing open-mouthed and horror-struck, shrieked at what she saw, and made for the door of the house. Every one began to move. They were prepared for scars, disfigurements, tangible horrors, but *nothing!* . . . For the man who stood there shouting some incoherent explanation, was a solid gesticulating figure up to the coat-collar of him, and then—nothingness, no visible thing at all!"

The Invisible Man was a big hit. The reviews were very favorable, critics having no objections to Wells's subject matter this time. Joseph Conrad, who was to become one of the great novelists of modern times, wrote Wells a flattering letter. "It is uncommonly fine," Conrad wrote. "Into this . . . you've managed to put an amazing quantity of effects. . . . I am always powerfully impressed by your work. Impressed is *the* word, O Realist of the Fantastic!"

Realist of the Fantastic. Conrad's phrase describes perfectly Wells's fictional methods and one of the reasons for the success of his scientific romances. Where other writers—notably Verne—were exuberant in their descriptions of marvels and wonders, Wells, in his fiction, took the marvels for granted. They were givens of the situations in his stories, and he described them realistically and economically. "Suspension of disbelief" is a phrase used to describe what happens to readers engaged with good fiction—they do not disbelieve the story, although they know it is not true. Wells's great gift, which Conrad recognized, was his ability to make readers not disbelieve in things that not only are not true but never could be true.

Wells succeeded at this in *The Invisible Man,* and the book remains readable and popular today. Wells himself remarked toward the end of his life that "to many young people nowadays I am just the author of *The Invisible Man.*"

Wells's talent for "fantastic realism" had served him well thorugh three novels—*The Time Machine, The Island of Doctor Moreau,* and *The Invisible Man.* Each of the novels focused upon a central character against fantastic backgrounds. The Time Traveller faced the world of the far future; Prendick faced Moreau and the Beast People; the Invisible Man faced a small village as well as his own inner nature.

Now Wells set himself a larger challenge. In his new scientific romance he would write of the entire world, of war, of invasion and global terror. And write not just of our world but of another world as well. The other world was Mars, and the story was called *The War of the Worlds.* It is, along with *The Time Machine,* one of his two most famous works.

The novel opens calmly, in the closing years of the nineteenth century. Quickly, though, the calm is shattered by the landings of spacecraft from Mars. The craft are filled with beings, and their appearance is one of the high points of the novel. Curious people have gathered around one of the spacecraft, and as they watch, it opens and one of its passengers is revealed.

"A big greyish rounded bulk, the size, perhaps, of a bear, was rising slowly and painfully out of the cylinder. As it bulged up and caught the light it glistened like wet leather.

"Two large dark-coloured eyes were regarding me steadfastly. The mass that framed them, the head of the thing, was rounded. . . . There was a mouth under the eyes, the lips of which quivered and panted, and dropped saliva. . . . A lank tentacular appendage gripped the edge of the cylinder, another swayed in the air.

"Those who have never seen a living Martian can scarcely imagine the strange horror of its appearance. The peculiar V-shaped mouth with its pointed upper lip, the absence of brow ridges, the absence of a chin beneath the wedgelike lower lip, the incessant quivering of this mouth, the Gorgon groups of tentacles, the tumultuous breathing of the lungs in a strange atmosphere, the evident heaviness and painfulness of each movement due to the greater gravitational energy of the earth—above all the extraordinary intensity of the immense eyes. . . ."

"Realist of the Fantastic" had never been so apt. Following their arrival, the Martians launched a reign of terror and destruction upon the earth. Wells greatly enjoyed writing the passages about the opening battles. He had discovered one of the small pleasures of being a writer of fiction. "I completely wreck and destroy Woking," he noted in a letter, "killing my neighbors in painful and eccentric ways—then proceed via Kingston and Richmond to London, which I sack, selecting South Kensington for feats of particular atrocity."

In the course of the novel Wells gives the reader a picture of an earth defeated, of London destroyed, of mankind without hope. But there is a hopeful ending, one which harks back once more to Wells's concern for science's responsibility to society.

Perhaps the most compelling of Wells's novels, *The War of the Worlds* was greeted enthusiastically. Wells had triumphed once again.

The War of the Worlds was the equivalent of a modern best-seller, and Wells's income rose even higher. He and Jane began looking for a more comfortable home. After years of working hunched over the dining room table, he was able to look for a house with a separate study.

And still he wrote. His next scientific romance, *When the Sleeper Wakes,* is little known today. It is a story of time travel, of a modern Rip Van Winkle who falls into a mysterious sleep and awakens in the twenty-second century. Written in 1897, *When the Sleeper Wakes* contains Wells's vision of the future—a world containing airplanes, television, enormous cities, and other fairly accurate forecasts. The happiness the sleeper perceives in this future world, though, is illusory, and he is plunged into intrigues and rebellion.

The book gave Wells a great deal of difficulty. He wrote passages again and again. "I'm having awful times with [*When the Sleeper Wakes*]. . . . It's gotten just at the top of my powers or a little beyond 'em!" he wrote to his friend novelist George Gissing. "I'm midway between a noble performance and a disaster."

Wells was tired. He had been working virtually without cease since *The Time Machine,* and the nonstop toil was at last beginning to take its toll. He needed a holiday; he was afraid of falling ill again.

Finally his ability to work failed him. In desperate need of escape, Wells "scamped the finish of *When the Sleeper Wakes.*" He rushed through the final chapters, sent them to his publisher, and began packing his bags for a trip to Europe.

On March 7, 1898, Wells and Jane left for Rome. Wells's

weariness had grown deeper. Exhaustion made him feel close to illness much of the time.

But at the same time he must have felt a certain contentment. He had come so far. Under his sure hand the scientific romance—*science fiction*—had become a legitimate field for serious literary work. Through science fiction Wells had risen from consumptive, unemployed teacher to popular novelist on the brink of even greater success. He and Jane had traveled from rented rooms and unfriendly landladies to a comfortable rented home in Worcester Park.

Wells, as he left for the Continent, was a respected young writer, critically acclaimed as well as financially successful. Despite his uncertainty about *When the Sleeper Wakes,* the response to his scientific stories had not diminished and showed no signs of doing so. Wells had a few more such books planned, but he was planning other types of work as well.

He still possessed, and would possess until the end of his life, a strong streak of childishness. Wells was capable of hard work over long hours, phenomenal discipline, but he was also easily bored. He could not be content simply as a science fiction writer. He had other things to say, things that could not be said in scientific romances.

He looked upon his journey to Europe not simply as an opportunity to visit new lands, but also as a chance to get back in touch with himself. It was an opportunity to get away from his writing desk and consider the shape he wished his career to assume.

He was not yet thirty-two years old, and already he had mastered time and space. He was almost universally regarded as the great master of the story of the future. Now, H. G. Wells was curious to see how well he could write about the present.

ELEVEN

NOVELIST

WELLS AND JANE SPENT an enjoyable two months touring Italy. Wells managed to relax a bit, and visited numerous friends, including George Gissing, the novelist to whom he'd grown close. Gissing, nine years older than Wells, had enjoyed none of his friend's success. Despite great talent, Gissing was not a popular novelist, and spent much of his life in slums, poor, despairing, bitter. Nevertheless, he and Wells got along comfortably, comparing their views of life and art.

By the time Wells returned to England he felt ready to take up his pen once more, although the trip had not rejuvenated him as he had hoped. He applied himself to a new novel, not a scientific romance but a story of ordinary people and ordinary events. The book was *Love and Mr. Lewisham,* and Wells had begun it before traveling abroad; he had been dissatisfied with it, and put it aside. Now, he tried again.

He worked hard, using all the craft he had, but he needed more than just craft. The book would not jell. Just weeks after returning to Worcester Park Wells was ready to leave again. He decided that he and Jane should spend some time at the seashore, and on July 29, 1898, they set off on their bicycles for Seaford, on the south coast of England.

They arrived early in August. Wells had not weathered the trip well. He ached and was running a fever. Even after settling down his health did not improve. His injured kidney was acting up again. Fortunately, one of the reasons for the trip was to visit a physician in New Romney who had asked them to stay with him. Now Jane wired ahead to ask if they might come to New Romney immediately.

Wells and Jane left Seaford by train and the journey, though much less taxing than bicycling, took much out of the young novelist. "I was now in considerable pain," he wrote later. "The jolting carriages seemed malignantly uncomfortable, I suffered from intense thirst, I could get nothing to drink and the journey was interminable."

Upon arriving at the doctor's home, Wells was put to bed and prepared for an operation. The surgery did not take place, for by the time he was in sufficient health to withstand the operation, Wells's kidney had stopped causing trouble. Bedrest and a healthy diet, as well as an avoidance of work, were the new prescriptions.

Wells spent many weeks in bed and during that time he did little writing. The one project he undertook was a present for the doctor's child. He worte a delightful story called *The Story of Tommy and the Elephant* (published years later as *The Adventures of Tommy*), illustrated with Wells's own drawings.

Wells's illness and recuperation caused much concern among his fellow writers. Wells was such a bundle of energy that his colleagues were distraught to hear of him confined to bed. George Gissing wrote that Herbert "*must* be his old self again . . ." and spoke of his debt to Wells's kindness and wit. Joseph Conrad wrote of how much he cared for Wells, and how much the illness concerned him.

One of the more touching expressions of concern for the invalid occurred when the great novelist Henry James and the literary philanthropist Edmund Gosse arrived on bicycles to visit Wells. James, by two decades Wells's senior, was revered as the great living master of the novel; his books had done much to pave the way for writers such as Wells, although James never enjoyed popular success. James and Gosse visited with Wells for a time, talking of literature, inquiring about Wells's health. It was not until later that Wells realized that the two men had called on him to offer financial assistance if it were needed.

It was not. Wells's bank balance was growing nicely, and as his health improved he began to consider purchasing a house. When his doctor told him that he needed to remain in a climate like that of the seacoast, Wells and Jane began looking at houses.

Finally they rented a home and there Wells threw himself into the final revision of *Love and Mr. Lewisham*. He was comfortable with the novel now, and felt that it was "an altogether more serious undertaking than anything I have done before."

Wells understood the characters of whom he wrote. *Love and Mr. Lewisham* is the story of a young schoolmaster who dreams of greater things. Like his creator, young Lewisham prepared a *schema,* a plan of study by which to get ahead in the world; like Wells, Lewisham served as assistant master of a small school. The similarities between author and character diverged when Lewisham fell in love. In the novel, after Lewisham's marriage, under pressure from the domestic demands of a family, the teacher gives up his dreams of a brighter future, and settles for a conventional existence.

His first real non-science-fiction novel, *Love and Mr. Lewisham* marked Wells's coming of age as a novelist. He captured details from observation rather than imagination, he told a moving and contemporary story of real people under believable pressures, and he dealt also with his own philosophical concerns.

The book was a success with the public, but the response of the critics was mixed. Some felt it the best thing he had done. Others felt that Wells should return to scientific romances. The critics were not alone. Arnold Bennett, an influential writer as well as a friend of Wells's, wrote to ask when Wells would return to the sorts of stories that had made him famous.

The question made Wells furious. He replied to Bennett immediately. "Why the Hell have you joined the conspiracy to restrict me to one type of story? I want to write novels and before God I *will* write novels."

He was serious. He knew that he could not make a lasting career from a single type of story. His temperament was too energetic, his mind too full of questions about too many things. He was not about to be restricted to one literary form, no matter what response he received. *Love and Mr. Lewisham* was merely the first novel about "real life" he had written. It would not be his last.

Still, he did return to science fiction in his next novel. Having written of the earth invaded by aliens, he now wrote of earthlings invading another world. He called the novel *The First Men in the Moon.*

In this novel Wells tells the story of a wonderful journey to the moon undertaken by Professor Cavor, who has perfected an element that frees men from gravity. Cavor, accompanied by Bedford, the story's narrator, prepares a vessel and sets out for the moon.

The voyage is an exciting one, filled with details of spaceflight that were astonishingly accurate, especially in Wells's description of weightlessness: "It was the strangest sensation conceivable, floating thus loosely in space . . . not disagreeable at all, exceedingly restful!" The passage ends with the narrator likening weightlessness to the beginning of a dream.

Upon delivering his heroes to the moon, Wells's prescience failed him, but not his storytelling ability. Science would reveal that the moon was a barren world, lifeless and without atmosphere. Wells's vision was fanciful and frightening, showing the reader a world that is dead only at night. When the sun shines on it the surface of the moon is covered with strange and beautiful life forms possessed of alien beauty. And inside the moon Cavor and Bedford discover a great civilization, that of the Selenites.

The First Men in the Moon delighted those readers who felt that Wells's great strength was as a writer of scientific romances. In fact, in later years there would be many who would argue that with the story of Cavor's journey to the moon, Wells wrote the last of his great cycle of science fiction novels.

If Wells knew that he had reached his pinnacle as a writer of scientific romances, he did not let it interrupt his other interests. He was dissatisfied with the rented house, and after some searching for another home, he decided that the only way to achieve satisfaction was to build his own home.

Wells approached the design of his house with the same enthusiasm and attention to detail he brought to his writing. Everything about the house should be modern and convenient. He engaged one of the most innovative architects of the day, Charles Voysey. Voysey was a man possessed of opinions equally as strong as Wells's, and throughout the design and planning stages their conversations trembled on the brink of argument as they went over the features that would be built into the house.

During the designing of the house Wells remained aware that he was not yet completely well. A relapse was possible and he took that into consideration. "The living-rooms were on one level with the bedrooms so that if I presently had to live in a wheeled chair I could be moved easily from room to room."

Another area in which Wells made his will known was in the decoration of the front door. Voysey wished to put his trademark, a heart, upon the door, but Wells refused. "I protested at wearing my heart so conspicuously outside," he wrote. "We compromised on a spade. We called the house Spade House."

At last the design was approved and construction began. Wells was as opinionated in the matter of building the house as he had been in its design. He hovered over the builders, offering unwanted and impractical advice, asking endless questions. The laborers did not seem to mind—they thought the author was another Wells, a man who was one of the great gamblers of the day!

But Spade House did get finished, and it was a lovely home that overlooked the sea. Its design and construction led Wells to think seriously about the future of homes. He was struck by the observation that many of the construction techniques used on Spade House were little different from those used in ancient times. He wrote a piece calling for great innovations in home-building: prefabrication and synthetic building materials were among his suggestions.

As far as the details inside homes of the future, his eye for progress and change was as clear as ever. Wells foresaw a day when homes would be air-conditioned and centrally heated with electricity, as well as equipped with more fanciful devices such as beds that made themselves.

Late in 1900 he and Jane moved into Spade House. Wells at last had a study of his own design, and he set to work in it, creating a new novel. It was not his only creation during those days. As he wrote to Arnold Bennett, "Mrs. Wells and I have been collaborating (and publication is expected in early July) in the invention of a human being."

Wells was going to be a father.

TWELVE

ANTICIPATOR

WELLS'S FIRST CHILD WAS born on July 17, 1901. The boy was named George Philip Wells, but he soon came to be known simply as "Gip."

From the first Gip delighted his father. Wells enjoyed being a parent, took great pleasure in devising games and stories and diversions for children. Perhaps he recalled his own not completely happy childhood too clearly; he wanted his children to enjoy their youth, to learn early the lessons that had come late to their father.

Jane had had a difficult time with the birth, and she was, for a while, confined to her bed to recover. She was cared for by nurses and servants, for her husband was not at home. While in many ways he and Jane seemed the perfect couple, Wells had learned that Jane was no closer to his ideal woman —one who was intellectual and physically passionate and re-sponsive—than Isabel had been. Jane was frail, and her inter-est in the physical aspects of marriage, which was never strong, seemed to dwindle after Gip's birth. She and Wells would have one more child, but their marriage would be essen-tially sexless for the rest of its life. They worked out an arrangement whereby Wells was given freedom to see other women, so long as he did not cause a scandal.

After Gip's birth Wells traveled through southern England. He had much on his mind. Having conquered the scientific romance to the point where any new story of science was compared to his works, and having made a good start on establishing himself as a serious novelist, he was eager for new fields of literary endeavor.

His head swam with ideas, hundreds of ideas and dozens of theories. He realized that there was more to life than literature, no matter how good a writer one might be. Wells began to seek involvement in the world beyond books.

Throughout 1901 he felt as though he had a fever, a fever for the future. His plans and schemes were not for new books, although there would be plenty of those, but for the future of mankind, the *real* future, not a literary creation. Wells wanted to apply his energy and talent to the creation of a better lot for humanity. Wells had worked with dedication and integrity to set forth his ideas in his scientific romances, but he knew that most people read those novels for their entertainment value alone. He wanted to try another path.

That path found its direction as a series of magazine articles in which Wells speculated seriously about the future. The articles may have seemed at first to be concerned with the mechanical and physical details of life in the days to come, but as always there were deeper meanings in Wells's words.

He had arrived at the conclusion that the twentieth century would be a turning point for civilization. The time was ripe for an overhaul of the way people lived, for putting the wonders and marvels of science to work for the benefit of all humanity. It was time to cast out all the old ways of doing things and arrive at new ways, ways suited to the construction of a more perfect world, a world approaching perfection.

As he wrote to a friend, Wells wanted "to undermine and destroy the monarch monogamy and respectability—and the British Empire—all under the guise of a speculation about motor cars and central heating."

Wells was not becoming a wild-eyed revolutionary by any means. But he was completely convinced that the fundamental nature of society would have to change drastically if the future of the world was to be bright. New ways must be designed to cope with the new world, just as he and Jane had arrived—not without pain, to be sure—at the new definition of their marriage. In fact, he had as many ideas about relationships as he did about "motor cars and central heating."

The articles were collected and published as a book in 1901. The book was called *Anticipations of the Reaction of Mechanical and Scientific Progress Upon Human Life and Thought.* For obvious reasons the book came generally to be known simply as *Anticipations.* Wells always considered it to be "the keystone to the main arch of my work." In the book he made the first systematic outline of his projections of the future.

Anticipations was unique. Readers were not quite certain what to make of this strange volume of speculations and guesses and suggestions. Once again Wells had broken new ground. "*Anticipations* was not only a new start for me, but, it presently became clear, a new thing in general thought. It may have been a feeble and vulnerable innovation, but it was as new as a new-laid egg. It was the first attempt to forecast the future as a whole. . . ."

The future as a whole! H. G. Wells could settle for no less! How could he content himself with a narrow corner of the small world of literature when he had a mind that embraced the entire future?

In *Anticipations* Wells began with a look at the effect of the steam engine upon transportation. He wrote of the effect of change, of the way in which change spread throughout society. From his starting point he guided the reader through a series of ever-larger projections. He forecast change in cities, new styles of family life, truly modern education. He urged a separation of sexuality from procreation, comparing sexuality once it was freed from old-fashioned and outdated morality to golf: a pleasant and harmless activity. In 1901 this was a startling and bold concept, and it retains its boldness in some circles today.

The culmination of the book was Wells's examination of the idea he considered the only hope for the survival of mankind: the World State. It was an idea that occupied him much of the time, although he had not yet come to grips with how a world state—a single government for all of humanity—might be brought about. He made a few suggestions in *Anticipations,* but the details continued to concern him.

Wells had outlined a plan for the future that was radical, exciting, and *new.* It struck a responsive chord with the reading public. Not even Wells had anticipated the reaction to his *Anticipations.* "Macmillan, my English publishers, were caught unawares by the demand and had sold out the first edition before they reprinted. It sold as well as a novel."

The book not only sent people scurrying to bookstores and libraries, it also served as a spark igniting vigorous debate. It was a popular topic of conversation among England's intelligentsia, among those who set the intellectual fashion for the day. Among them was Beatrice Webb, a serious and dedicated socialist who would soon figure largely in Wells's life. She wrote favorably of *Anticipations,* feeling it to be a remarkable book and recommending serious study of it.

Not everyone agreed; one newspaper called the book a "travesty." Wells's friend Joseph Conrad also had some objections. Conrad thought that the ideas Wells put forth were too strict, that the world would have to bring itself into line with Wells's ideas in order for the future as forecast in the book to come about. Conrad urged that Wells should reverse his tack, should become a part of the world rather than inviting the world to become a part of his vision.

Wells took Conrad's criticism without complaint. In fact, concerned about his friend's bank balance, he secretly helped to get Conrad an assignment for magazine articles criticizing Wells's work.

The effect of *Anticipations* was perhaps best expressed in the *Westminster Gazette,* which suggested that the book served more as an explosive than a document, blasting away the "conventional, acquiescent, complacent frame of mind" that for so long had been a hallmark of English society.

English society was not alone in being struck by the audacity of *Anticipations.* The book was as successful and controversial in Europe as it had been in Wells's homeland. Such widespread success reaffirmed Wells's belief: He had found an effective way to reach his audience and to make his message known.

Wells did not fail to take advantage of his increasing fame and influence. "Among other people who were excited by *Anticipations* was myself. I became my own first disciple. I was writing the human prospectus."

Another result of his success with the book was that Wells, who had failed at the Normal School, was now asked to deliver a lecture at the Royal Institution, where some of the great scientists of the day gathered. Wells was elated and set to work to make his lecture an effective follow-up to *Anticipations.*

For long hours he worked over his talk, planning his points, thinking through his argument. He called the lecture "The Discovery of the Future." He knew what points he wanted to make, and before that august body he made them clearly.

"I drew a hard distinction between what I called the legal (past regarding) and the creative (future regarding) minds," he wrote later. "I insisted that we overrated the darkness of the future, that by adequate analysis of contemporary processes its conditions could be brought within the range of our knowledge and its form controlled . . . that mankind was at the dawn of a great change-over from life regarded as a system of consequences to life regarded as a system of constructive effort."

It was this attitude that separated Wells from many of the social critics of his time. Wells was not content simply to criticize; he offered alternatives. He showed his audiences ways in which criticism could be turned into new construction. He was well aware that to look to the future with nothing but optimism was not only foolish but also dangerous. Nonetheless, he refused to give himself over completely to pessimism. Humans were gifted, Wells felt, they were *special*; they could be great, they could make for themselves and their descendants a great future.

Of course, for that future to come about all would have to follow the prescriptions offered by "Doctor" Herbert George Wells. Joseph Conrad had a point with his critique of *Anticipations*. Wells himself soon learned that there lay a great distance between exciting the public with bold speculations, and persuading the public to follow your instructions. It was one thing for a person to give up the small price of a book, another thing entirely to call for that person to give up his or her way of life in return for the promise of a better future.

For the time being, though, Wells found himself at the center of attention. After *Anticipations* he was deluged with requests for lectures, articles, books. The response was even greater than for his scientific romances. Everyone, it seemed, wanted to hear the predictions of the young writer. Wells had never before been so busy. The study at Spade House became the source of an almost ceaseless torrent of short pieces and books, lectures and pamphlets, stories and novels. And every piece was alive with Wells's energy, alive with his arguments for his new world.

"The Discovery of the Future" was published as a separate pamphlet. Close on its heels followed another pamphlet, *Life and Thought*. In these brief works Wells amplified his arguments for the liberation of mankind from drudgery and outmoded ways of life. He called passionately for conscious effort toward the creation of a world government.

Through all of this new work and notoriety, Wells managed to produce some fiction. He even wrote a novel, although it was a slight one. *The Sea Lady* told a whimsical and romantic story about a mermaid.

No sooner was the mermaid out of the way than Wells returned to his predictions. *Mankind in the Making*, a full-length follow-up to *Anticipations*, was published in 1903. In the new volume Wells dealt once more with pressing questions concerning the future of education, housing, government, and so on. *Mankind in the Making* had a more strident tone than its predecessor, not so much telling what could be, but rather preaching what must be done. Conrad had warned him but Wells had not listened. He had fallen into the trap so common to self-proclaimed prophets: He was taking himself too seriously.

Wells later came to understand his error, referring to *Mankind in the Making* as "revivalism . . . field preaching." He felt that he had yet to understand fully his own ideas, and was even further from arriving at a means of translating those ideas into concrete, worldwide action.

But he kept trying. And his ideas for the future grew far grander than any he had set forth in his scientific romances. He decided that it did not matter that he had no means of translating these ideas into reality. That would come later. It had to: His ideas were too valuable not to receive a practical test in the world. It was simply a matter of time.

While waiting for the practical test to arrive, though, Wells continued to refine and expand his scheme for the world to come. His ideas, radical in the beginning, now crept toward the edge of the dangerous. Wells proposed that society be divided into two segments: those who were going to design and build the future, and those who would simply serve in it until their weaknesses were bred out of the race. This was—and remains—frightening speculation, approaching the sort of rules Hitler and others have sought to impose.

Of course Wells did not see his vision as totalitarian. His aim was not the attainment of personal power, but quite simply the salvation of the human race. He considered and rejected a "selective breeding" program. He did not want to eliminate but to build. What Wells proposed "building" was a new race of superior beings, a race of people better than ourselves, a race equal to the challenges of the magnificent new world he envisioned.

Whether or not he thought of Doctor Moreau as he made his plans is not known. That story had contained strong warnings about the sort of alterations Wells gave thought to now. But he could not let the idea alone.

When *Mankind in the Making* did not receive the acclaim that had greeted *Anticipations,* Wells decided to put some of his ideas into a piece of fiction. He undertook a new scientific romance, and in late 1903 he produced *The Food of the Gods,* which was published the following year.

More openly satirical than his earlier books, *The Food of the Gods* told the story of a special food that dramatically increased the growth of anything that ate it. The world was soon overrun by giant insects and babies, enormous rats, everything grown beyond its normal size.

Giant babies! In Wells's hands the problem of oversized infants was food for humor as well as thought. Obviously, for a giant child, a normal baby carriage would not do. "By the time this baby was twelve months old he measured just one inch under five feet. . . . They had an invalid's chair to carry him up and down to his nursery, and his special nurse, a muscular young person just out of training, used to take him for his airings in a Panhard 8 h.p. hill-climbing-perambulator specially made to meet his requirements."

Humor soon gave way to moralizing and Wells smothered his story with philosophy. Governments, he was saying, are no longer able to keep pace with the rate of change in the modern world. Problems grow too rapidly. Everything happens faster than it used to, and the only things that have not changed are those institutions that most desperately need to.

Wells's own life was changing in 1903. That year saw the birth of his and Jane's second child, another boy: Frank Richard Wells. The presence of two children in Spade House spurred Wells to frequent and deep thought on the nature of education. What was the purpose of education? he asked himself. What was the right sort of education? At what age should education begin?

Education, as Wells saw it, was the path upon which mankind would walk into the new world. If there was any one element that was the cornerstone of his philosophy it was the necessity of universal education. Wells recalled his own childhoood too clearly. He remembered how many of the young men he'd known received only enough education to prepare them for lives as clerks, draper's assistants, and small businessmen. He also remembered the wonders he had discovered in books, the new worlds those books opened to him, and he grew more determined than ever to do what he could to spread the gospel of education throughout his country and the world.

He sought once more to combine his speculations on education and government with a scientific romance. The new book was called *A Modern Utopia* and in it Wells tried another strategy. Rather than presenting the sort of changes that would bring about a new world, in *A Modern Utopia* he wrote of that world as though it were already a reality.

Utopia. Defined as places ruled by absolute perfection in laws, government, and social order, utopias of various descriptions had been created by many writers. Utopian fiction is a respected tradition in literature, with many books, poems, and plays presenting ideas and theories for how such a world should run.

Every utopia must be ruled for the common good. In some utopian works, this rule is achieved through complete democracy. Other utopias were described as benevolent dictatorships, governed by a minority of persons who hold the rights and interests of all citizens to heart. Wells's utopia was of the second type.

A Modern Utopia, which appeared in 1905, shared with most utopian literature characters who were not of the utopian world but of our own. In Wells's book two men had gone for a walk and suddenly found themselves in a new world. The world was like our own, except that it was structured around utopian ideals, which were, of course, the ideals of H. G. Wells.

To rule this perfect world Wells suggested an elite order known as the Samurai, taking their name from the highly disciplined Japanese aristocracy of warriors. Wells's Samurai were not warriors but rather a class apart from mankind. The Samurai in Wells's utopia were the most intelligent, most morally upright and honorable people in the utopian world. Anyone could become a Samurai, Wells proposed, if they could pass the difficult qualifying examinations.

In *A Modern Utopia* Wells suggested that society be divided into four classes of people: the kinetic, who took action and ruled the world; the poetic, who contributed imagination and creativity; the dull, who were the workers; and the base, who were the lowest element of society. It was ironic that Wells, so defiant of his mother's "proper order of society," would develop an order far more rigid than the one to which Sarah clung. Wells, though, did not see the irony.

He felt that the old order—the order of the Victorian Age —was maintained simply through inertia. There was no change because people were too cowardly and too lazy to change themselves. It was far easier simply to let things run along as they had always run along, patching problems here, making temporary repairs there, but avoiding a coherent and complete attempt to revitalize society.

Wells knew that if such revitalization were to be brought about it would be accomplished by those who were willing and able to take action. The "common man" had little interest in revamping the world, Wells felt. He thought of his father. Joseph Wells was a dreamer, a man who had chased several schemes for wealth and happiness, a man of some ambition. But Joseph Wells—and others like him—would be far more willing to apply themselves to the pursuit of success in the world they knew, rather than risk the long struggle required to create a new order. It was natural for most people to feel that way, Wells realized, but that did not mean that the new world could not be obtained.

Wells came to believe that rule *of* all the people, *by* all the people, could not continue as a viable form of government. Most people did not know enough or care enough to take an intelligent stand in determining the future of their world.

"We want the world ruled, not by everybody," Wells wrote in an attempt to sum up his feelings, "but by a politically minded organization open, with proper safeguards, to everybody." In short: rule *of* all the people who cared enough to *work* for good government, *by* all the people who were able and willing to bear the burdens of government.

What Wells understood, though, was that the creation of such an order was not something people were willing to give their time and efforts to. The average man or woman would happily read of H. G. Wells's plans for the future, would discuss and argue his positions, would applaud him as he stood upon a lecture stage. But those same people felt that Wells's ideas were finally only the stuff of scientific romances and exciting articles in popular magazines, not ideas actually called for here on earth. At least not for hundreds, maybe thousands, of years.

"I realized that an Order of the Samurai was not a thing which comes about of itself, and if ever it were to exist, it must be realized as the result of a very deliberate effort." He set himself to that effort, and it became one of the guiding concerns of his life.

And soon his determination to bring his literary creation into actual existence would embroil him in a bitter battle with some of the foremost intellectual names of his time.

THIRTEEN

FIGHTING FABIAN

THROUGH ALL OF HIS work at global plans and prescriptions, Wells never forgot that he was a novelist. It was with fiction that he made his reputation, and fiction remained to him in many ways the most important of all his writings. He knew that works such as *Anticipations* had engaged his philosophical and argumentative nature in ways novels never could. But he also knew that his nonfiction did little for his artistic reputation and position. His nonfiction was lecture, pure exposition of ideas, in which form and style mattered less than content. Fiction demanded more: In a novel he must subordinate (or try to) his lectures to his story, he must concentrate on the creation of believable characters, he must pursue *art* rather than simply *idea*.

It was a great challenge and one Wells felt up to. He thought that he had it in him to create great novels, books that would capture their times, and also serve as literature that would outlive their author. Wells's friend Henry James thought Wells had a great future as a novelist. He urged Wells to spend more time on his novels, to approach them as James himself might. James believed that the purpose of art was to give shape to life, not merely reproduce life. James labored over his novels, giving careful thought to every sentence, using his art to create a vision of life upon which the judgments and tastes of Henry James had been imposed.

While Wells was flattered to have the attention of the Master, as James was known, Wells already knew that the slow and painstaking creation of artistic masterpieces would not be his way. He had too much to say and was too eager to say it. Wells's stories rushed out at great speed, and rather than spending time on them in search of aesthetic perfection, Wells would turn to his next project, his mind already two steps ahead of his pen.

Nevertheless he did pursue art, and in 1905 published a novel that had occupied him, on and off, for seven years. In fact, the book was begun on October 5, 1898, the same day he completed *Love and Mr. Lewisham,* the first of his "serious" novels. Wells recorded the event—birth of one book, conception of another—in one of his humorous "picshuas." The novel begun that day came to be known as *Kipps.*

Kipps: The Story of a Simple Soul, to give its full title, is a novel whose roots lie deep in Wells's own life. Artie Kipps is a young man whose journey through life takes him to schools similar to those Wells attended, and who is apprenticed to a draper at an early age. Like his creator, Artie Kipps sought a means of overcoming the circumstances of his life and rising above them.

Wells gave the story a great deal of attention, repeatedly working his way through passages during the seven-year gestation of the book. Published within a few months of *A Modern Utopia, Kipps* made clear to the public that Wells was a writer of range and great talent. Even the Master was impressed. "They have left me prostrate with admiration," Henry James wrote of the two books. "I am lost in amazement at the diversity of your genius."

Yet James would once more go on to urge Wells to slow down, to take the time to impose form upon his work, rather than breathlessly telling a story.

Wells had no time to slow down. His theory of the novel

differed from James's. Wells did not see the novel as a work of art to be judged by its virtues and failures as art; Wells saw the novel as a vehicle for many things. Storytelling, entertainment, was certainly among the things Wells sought in his novels; he also wanted to get his messages across. In Artie Kipps, Wells portrayed the struggle to rise above one's origin, the pursuit of a better world. *Kipps* was a popular success, and its popularity did not diminish as years passed. In 1967, more than six decades after it was published, *Kipps* served as the basis for a musical motion picture, *Half a Sixpence.*

But musical motion pictures lay far in the future, and so did the revolution that so preoccupied Wells even as he finished *Kipps.* Art would have to wait. He knew that his Order of Samurai was a good and necessary idea, but he was not certain how to transform that idea into reality.

And then he encountered the Fabians.

In 1884 a society was founded in London whose purpose was to bring about some of the changes that Wells would crystallize on paper years later. The society was called the Fabian Society, after the Roman general Quintus Fabius Maximus. Fabius gained great fame for his brilliant strategies, which primarily consisted of harrying his enemies, irritating them, chipping away at them but never engaging them in actual battle. He wore them down gradually.

That was also the strategy of the Fabian Society. Founded by people who were committed to the ideal of a socialist state, the society's purpose was to bring that state into being through *gradual* changes in society. This policy of slow and steady reform was in opposition to the communist policy of revolution for social change. Rather than revolution, the Fabians believed in evolution.

One of the leading members of the Fabians was a young journalist named George Bernard Shaw. Shaw would become one of the great playwrights of the English language, and was as much a social critic as H. G. Wells. During the early years of the Fabian Society, however, Shaw was a struggling writer living in circumstances not unlike Wells's before *The Time Machine*. Wells and Shaw knew each other, in fact, and had reviewed plays together before success overtook them. They came to develop a friendly rivalry, and the opposition of two such powerful minds was often electric.

Joining George Bernard Shaw at the heart of the Fabians were Sidney and Beatrice Webb. Sidney Webb had been sought out by Shaw because of his great factual knowledge. Shaw felt that a precise mind was needed to offset the Fabian tendency to spend too much time theorizing, too little time working in the "real world." Sidney Webb's first Fabian book, *Facts for Socialists*, was printed originally in 1887, and went through printings and revisions and updatings until the end of World War II. Knowledge, Sidney Webb felt, was the key to a successful campaign for reform; an educated public would seek, and even embrace, reform.

Beatrice Webb, Sidney's wife, came from an upper-class background. Despite coming from a family of some wealth she became at an early age an active campaigner for reform. Her intelligence and insight were much prized by the Fabians, and along with her husband she served as the organization's intellectual heart.

In the closing years of the nineteenth century the Webbs and Shaw guided the Fabians to ever-greater influence. By the turn of the century, at the time *Anticipations* appeared, Fabian influence was being felt throughout English government. The Fabian plan called for this influence to spread and grow, slowly at first, with early decisions laying the groundwork for later ones until all reforms were accomplished. Evolution rather than revolution.

When *Anticipations* appeared, it caught the attention of the Fabians. Like other readers they were excited by Wells's bold vision of the future. Sidney Webb wrote Wells a note offering praise along with some gentle criticism. Webb felt that Wells concentrated too much on machines and not enough on people.

In her diary Beatrice Webb called *Anticipations* "the most remarkable book of the year." She, along with her husband, found Wells an intriguing writer.

A meeting was arranged. Wells and Jane got along well with the Webbs. Wells found himself invited again and again to Fabian gatherings. It was as though he were being courted. He listened carefully at these meetings and began to have some Fabian ideas of his own.

It struck him that the Fabians—a group already well established—might be just the means through which to bring about his reorganization of the world, his New Republic. Could it be that the Fabians might form the nucleus for a real Order of Samurai?

As for the Fabians themselves, they began to see Wells as an effective propagandist for their own causes.

H. G. Wells became a member of the Fabian Society in February 1903.

It was an interesting time for so strong-willed an individual to find himself part of the Fabians. A power struggle was taking place. Like many organizations, the Fabians found that success brought more problems than failure. As they gained more and more influence during the waning years of the last century, the Fabians began to argue and quarrel among themselves. Some Fabians felt that the society was fine, and that it should hold to the principles around which it was founded: slow and steady change through influencing existing institutions. Other members, however, felt that with the arrival of the new century, the time had come for the Fabians to break with existing political parties and form their own socialist political party.

Wells, driven by his incorrigible tendency to perceive himself as the center of any group he was with, saw the division of the Fabians as a problem awaiting *his* solution. He did not immediately seek to impose his ideas upon the society, but he did take an active part in its functions from his first days as a member. He was building a base.

One of his responsibilities was speechmaking. Wells was a poor public speaker. In later years he recalled himself "speaking haltingly on the verge of the inaudible, addressing my tie through a cascade moustache that was no sort of help at all, correcting myself as though I were a manuscript under treatment, making ill-judged departures into parenthesis. . . ."

Although no speaker, Wells did get his ideas across. He presented and championed them at Fabian meetings. He churned out pamphlets and articles and books in which he grew more and more determined to drive home the concerns that obsessed him. A world state, Wells expounded at every turn, a single government ruling the world, was the only answer to the problems that beset humanity. As early as *A Modern Utopia*, Wells understood that the concept of nations was being made obsolete by advances in communication and transportation. Utopia, he knew, would have to take in the whole world or it could not be.

Wells intended to forge from the basis of the Fabian Society the foundation of his New Republic, to create living Samurai, rather than paper ones. He discovered that he had little use for the classical methods of persuasion and patience by which the Fabians worked. Wells was ready for a little more action. In fact, he was desperate for it. Couldn't the Fabians see how urgent the need for global reform was? It was not enough to try to come to power in England, and wait and wait to come to power elsewhere. Change was needed, change must be immediate! Wells wanted to stir things up, to force the Fabians into a stronger offensive, to create debate and argument, to spread the gospel of socialism—as interpreted by Wells—and world government as rapidly as the gospel could be spread. Where the Fabians wanted civilized discourse, Wells wanted to shout at the top of his lungs.

He got some attention. One of the methods he used to attract the eyes and ears of a large audience was his frank (for the times) discussion of sexual matters. This was a bold and somewhat risky course to pursue in the years just after the passing of staid Queen Victoria, but Wells pressed on, undeterred, and perhaps even delighted, by the outrage his arguments sparked in some quarters.

It was not all outrage. England's young people were eager to move quickly beyond the repressive world of Queen Victoria's reign—the only world that their parents, people such as Sarah Wells, had known. And as with all young people whatever the era, their way of doing so was to cast aside the beliefs cherished and clung to by their parents. These young people dressed differently, they enjoyed new and innovative styles in music and theater, they chased eagerly after new ideas. And nobody's ideas were newer than H. G. Wells's.

Some of these young people became Fabians, and it was the younger Fabians who rallied behind Wells. They listened avidly to his complaints that the Fabian Society was too concerned with minor details, not possessed of enough vision for the task it had undertaken. Wells grow angry when he reflected upon the accomplishments of the Fabians. They spent all their time working quietly for small reforms in trivial matters such as water supply and gas regulation. They spent too little time considering that, had they only the will, they could build themselves into an organization that would shape the nature of the future. The time had come, Wells proposed, for the Fabian Society's membership to number in the voluble thousands, rather than the meek hundreds.

George Bernard Shaw and the Webbs watched with no little interest as Wells's influence in the society grew throughout 1905. They read this pamphlet *The Faults of the Fabian* and winced at its charges that the society served no real purpose, that its accomplishments were minor and would have come about even without the Fabians. They listened to Wells as he maintained that the time for compromise was over, that the time had arrived for action. And they discussed among themselves Wells's growing influence in the society. It was becoming clear that Wells intended to seize control of the Fabians for himself.

Those who had been with the organization longest were not about to let Wells take over without a fight. Throughout the winter of 1905–1906 the two factions wrangled over one point of procedure or another. Wells won some arguments and he lost some. In the course of the struggle, though, he managed, with his inimitable style, to offend nearly everyone involved. Shaw and the Webbs began to suspect that Wells was more interested in spinning his plans for the society, in working to take it over, than he was in actually leading it.

An interruption in the debate arrived in March 1906, in the forms of Wells's first trip to the United States. He was excited about the journey, and asked Henry James to provide him with letters of introduction to interesting and typical Americans. Wells's curiosity was boiling once again: Could America be the land of the future about which he so often wrote?

The American trip was to be underwritten by a series of articles Wells would write for the London *Tribune*. In addition, it struck Wells that he might use the journey to his advantage by increasing the American reading public's awareness of him and his works. He was popular in the United States but was not yet the celebrity there that he had become in his homeland.

So it was with a variety of purposes that he said farewell to Jane and the children, and boarded the liner *Carmania* on March 27, 1906.

He spent two months in the United States. In addition to writing articles, he gave lectures and allowed himself to be honored at universities and literary societies. He met with some American socialists and compared their organization, efforts, and accomplishments with those of the Fabians in his own country.

Wells also spent some time at the White House, meeting and enjoying conversation with President Theodore Roosevelt. The "Rough Rider" was exactly the sort of man Wells admired most—given to optimism and vision, driven by a burning and unquenchable ambition to *get things done.* Roosevelt spoke admiringly of *The Time Machine.* The president knew the book well, and its underlying pessimism did not bother him. Sitting with Wells in the gardens of the White House, he pointed out his opinion that the Morlocks and the deevolution of society did not matter *now.* What mattered now was beginning the effort to stave off deevolution, with continuing to *try* to build a new and more harmonious world.

In *The Future in America,* the book he made of his *Tribune* articles, Wells wrote that Theodore Roosevelt in 1906 was perhaps the most daring thinker in political power. Such a man gave Wells hope for the future of his dreams.

In late May Wells returned to England, and to the struggle for control of the Fabian Society. Shaw and the Webbs had taken advantage of Wells's absence to consider their position. It was becoming obvious that Wells would settle for nothing less than their capitulation to him as leader of the Fabians. Wells had no use for compromise. The established members of the organization feared that the Fabians were merely an indulgence for Wells. He offered few hard solutions for the problems the organization faced, promising only that if his advice were taken, all would soon be better.

It was an interesting time. Wells was approaching forty. Sarah Wells, her son's link to the past, had died in 1905, enfeebled by an accident, her mind returning to Atlas House. Wells had children of his own now—children who, Jane pointed out, saw too little of their father. His youth was passing into middle age. He had aged out of his comfortable role as brash newcomer to English letters. He found himself a respected, if controversial, writer. Wells had written little fiction since *Kipps,* was embroiled in a struggle for power, was learning to deal with the guilt brought on by his increasingly frequent absences. In the midst of these varying demands and annoyances he returned to the scientific romance.

In the Days of the Comet was the new book's title, and the book was one of Wells's most controversial. In it Wells combined his flair for the romance with his speculative ability, and added for good measure his reflections about the issues that were dividing the Fabian Society, along with arguments closely related to his sexual situation.

In the novel a comet approaches earth, and the world is drastically changed as a result of exposure to the comet's vapors. The vapors do much of the work that Wells wanted the Fabian Society—or his Samurai—to do. The vapors transform a world of bitterness and warfare into a world of love and cooperation. The vapors also alter morality: The idea of monogamy disappears, and is replaced by "free love."

Wells was attempting to come to terms with his own unusual marital situation. He sought in his new novel to come to terms with the relationship he and Jane had arranged. "Free love" was his attempt to present a vision of physical love that was not linked to morality, but rather allowed men and women to enjoy sexual relations outside of marriage or with others than their marital partners.

Angry reaction set in immediately. Wells had gone too far. The *Times Literary Supplement* charged that, according to Wells, "Socialist men's wives . . . are, no less than their goods, to be held in common. . . . One wonders . . . what the other Fabians will say."

They said plenty. The linking of Fabian ideals with what seemed to many immoral ideas did not go over well with the established members of the society. With the young, the "Fabian Nursery" as they called themselves, Wells's ideas were a hit. In fact, he enjoyed romantic relationships with more than one young Fabian woman, and the gossip about his affairs was beginning to build.

Soon after publication of *In the Days of the Comet,* and while it was still surrounded by controversy, Wells spoke to a gathering of Fabians. The meeting was larger than usual, the audience swelling because of the excitement about H. G. Wells. He was sure to say something shocking.

Wells did not disappoint his audience. It was not enough to have economic freedom, he proclaimed, there must also be moral freedom. Women must be emancipated not only in terms of employment and voting, they must also be given freedom of love. The responsibility of the socialist was to free the world not just from oppression, but also from jealousy and possessiveness.

The tide began to turn against Wells. He had gone too far. A good many Fabians who had been his supporters broke with him on the issue of free love. They felt that sex and politics, morality and politics, love and jealousy and politics, were all unrelated, and that politics alone should be the focus of the Fabian Society. Wells by now was committed to his daring course. It wasn't just politics. It wasn't just economics. It wasn't just equality of employment and property. It was all of it. Every aspect of human life was connected. There could be no new world unless *everything* about the old world was revamped.

Wells wrote an article called "Socialism and the Family," in which some of his arguments were presented. The article was rejected by the Fabians. Shaw insisted that Wells learn to compromise, to work *with* others rather than dictating to them. Sidney and Beatrice Webb visited Wells and Jane, and left with the impression that Wells was growing bored with the society but was unwilling to give up his bid for leadership.

By the end of 1906 the matter was approaching an end. Wells's attempt to gain control was both blatant and determined. Equally determined were the Webbs and Shaw that

Wells play a part in the society but that moderation rule the day. Public debates were called for concerning Wells's demand for immediate reform of the Fabian Society.

The debates were held. Wells spoke for his side, and his poor stage presence cost his position some support. Then George Bernard Shaw, who was as gifted with his tongue as he was with his pen, stood and took Wells's proposals apart point by point. It was clear in minutes that Shaw had won the audience. Wells's proposal was defeated. The Fabian Society would change, but it would change at its own rate, in its own ways. Wells would have to forge his Samurai from other sources.

Wells lingered on in the Fabian Society for some time longer, attending meetings, making speeches. But his heart was no longer in the organization. He had had his opportunity and it had not gone his way. Wells was not a bad loser, but he was not a particularly good one. It would be years before he realized that it was his attitude as much as his opinions that cost him his influence with the Fabians.

As he grew older he would see "that I can be quite silly and inept; but no part of my career rankles so acutely in my memory with the conviction of bad judgment, gusty impulse and real inexcusable vanity, as that storm in a Fabian teacup. . . . I antagonized Shaw and Beatrice Webb, for example, by my ill-minded aggressiveness, yet both these people have since shown that their trend of mind is all towards just such a qualification of crude democracy [a restructured world] as in 1906 I was so clumsily seeking. I was fundamentally right and I was wrong-headed."

But it is of such mistakes that great lessons are learned, and H. G. Wells was never one to miss an opportunity for learning. His involvement with the Fabian Society was one of the key adventures in his life, and it taught him that he was perhaps not meant to have influence in traditional ways. Committees and quorums and debates were not for him. He was a writer, a novelist, and a prophet, and that was a route that could best be taken on one's own. The Fabians would find their way and Wells would find his. He would remain in contact with many of them for the rest of his life. He would have a love affair with one of the younger Fabians, which would cause a scandal. He would never forget his attempt to create in reality the ruling group he had conceived on paper.

His failure as a Fabian did not deter him from his attempt to remake the world. That impulse burned within him brighter than ever.

Nor did the commercial failure of *In the Days of the Comet* cause him to doubt his abilities as a writer of fiction. In fact, even as he was ending his career as a Fabian, Wells was wrestling onto the page the novel that many still consider to be his finest contribution to literature.

FOURTEEN

THE VISION DARKENS

Tono-Bungay. What an odd name for a book. *Tono-Bungay.* What a fine name for the book Wells wrote.

Tono-Bungay itself is a medicine, invented by Edward Ponderevo. Tono-Bungay works wonders, and Ponderevo is ready to spread the gospel of his miracle elixir. A modern man, Ponderevo knows just how to get his message across. *Advertising!*

"THE SECRET OF VIGOR, TONO-BUNGAY" a sign proclaims. Tono-Bungay also provides "HEALTH, BEAUTY, AND STRENGTH." It is a miracle elixir and soon there are other products: "'. . . a special adaptation containing eleven per cent of absolute alcohol . . . Tono-Bungay Hair Stimulant . . . Concentrated Tono-Bungay for the eyes . . . Tono-Bungay Lozenges . . . Tono-Bungay Chocolate . . .'"

Tono-Bungay conquered the world!

Unfortunately, Tono-Bungay was nothing more than a promise; it could work no miracles. This story of Edward Ponderevo's rise and fall—told by his nephew, George—comes closer to being a true masterpiece than any of Wells's other non-science-fiction novels. Wells spent four years constructing *Tono-Bungay,* shaping the book even as he was failing to shape the Fabian Society.

Wells put everything he had into the novel; it is in many

ways the richest book of his career. Its opening chapters tell the story of George Ponderevo's youth—as a boy unwillingly apprenticed to a draper by a mother employed at a large country house. Young George goes on to study science, fails his examinations, joins his uncle in the promotion of Tono-Bungay.

The novel also contains some elements of the scientific romance, dealing with aeronautics, radioactivity, and a search for a mineral known as "quap." *Tono-Bungay* even contains some examples of Wells's "picshuas."

Wells knew what he had accomplished in the book. He would speak of *Tono-Bungay* as "my most ambitious novel." It would be his last attempt to compose a work of fiction that aproached Henry James's criteria for literary art. Art for art's sake simply was not Wells's way. The urge to lecture was too deeply a part of him. "I shall never come as near to a deliberate attempt upon the novel as I did in *Tono-Bungay*," he would write in his autobiography.

Tono-Bungay was recognized from the moment of publication as a major achievement. Wells turned from it to another look at the future, a grim glimpse of the day after tomorrow. This was *The War in the Air*, published in 1908.

The War in the Air and Particularly How Mr. Bert Smallways Fared While It Lasted told the story of Bert Smallways's adventures in a balloon. While airborne, Smallways witnesses the destruction of the modern world, viewing a German aerial attack upon New York City, the escalation of the war, the final collapse of civilization.

The War in the Air was written in 1907, just four years after the Wright brothers flew at Kitty Hawk. Aircraft were still novelties, their virtue as weapons untested. But H. G. Wells saw their possibilities. "I . . . reasoned that air warfare, by making warfare three dimensional, would abolish the war front and with that the possibility of distinguishing between civilian and combatant or of bringing a war to a conclusive end," he wrote. Everyone would suffer when the next war erupted. There would be no hope for anyone.

Few people listened. *The War in the Air* was another crackerjack scientific romance, nothing more. There was just no way to beat old H. G. Wells when it came to spinning a yarn about crazy ideas—time machines and going to the moon, Martians, and now airplanes dropping bombs!

In Spade House Wells began to realize that the rest of the world was not unlike the Fabians. People were interested in hearing what he had to say, but were unwilling to take action to correct the problems he pointed out. He had failed to transform the Fabians into Samurai, and the great plans he presented in his books went unheeded. What was he doing wrong?

Wells knew the answer. He was doing nothing wrong. He lived in a complex world; people were distracted, too concerned with their individual and local problems to worry about the rest of society. Leave the state of the world to the politicians, let us alone, let us lead our lives—these were the attitudes held by most people, then as now.

The solution had to lie elsewhere. Or maybe not—Wells was beginning to believe that there was no solution. He began to consider another course. People would not listen because by the time they were old enough to take action they had already been trapped by the old ways. They grew mired in the same petty concerns and trivialities that had captured their parents and grandparents and all their ancestors. It was the same trap that caught and ultimately destroyed all civilizations.

The status quo. The way things are. The nature of life. Those were the traps, and they were especially annoying to Wells, who had fought against existing orders all his life.

Wells had the status quo much on his mind, for he was making a bold and scandalous assault upon it even as *Tono-*

Bungay and *The War in the Air* were being published. Wells was deeply involved with a young woman, Amber Reeves, and his involvement with her was shocking not only the status quo of literary London, but also the life of the Wells household.

Amber Reeves was a young Fabian whose vitality and enthusiasm for reform had captured Wells's imagination. He attempted to keep his relationship with Amber quiet, knowing that his behavior could disgrace Jane and his children if it became known. In April 1909 Amber revealed to Wells that she was pregnant with his child and, in a fit of exuberance and uncertainty, Wells and Amber left England for a trip to France.

Wells's domestic status quo had closed in upon him, and the affair with Amber was his way of seeking escape. He did not see why he should be bound to traditional morality when his own ideas of right and wrong were so much more appealing. In an attempt to legitimize his and Amber's child, however, he offered to marry her, but Amber was unwilling to be the cause of Wells's divorcing Jane.

Finally the hopelessness of the situation became clear to Wells. He could not lead two lives, one with Jane and the children, the other with Amber. A marriage was arranged between Amber and a young man she had known for years. Wells continued to see Amber socially after her marriage.

It was in fiction that the ideas behind his affair with Amber Reeves were explored by Wells. His next novel was *Ann Veronica,* and it told the story of a young woman who does not feel bound by conventional morality. Little in the book would seem shocking today, but Ann Veronica Stanley's willingness and enthusiasm to live with a man out of wedlock were shocking to readers in 1909. A cry went out that *Ann Veronica* must be banned.

Wells had done it again. His affair with Amber had

caused an uproar among his friends; his novel about a similar affair sparked an uproar across England.

Ann Veronica was denounced as "poisonous." Those who denounced it, though, admitted that there was nothing crude or pornographic about the novel. What they objected to were the *ideas* that underlay the story.

Wells made a public response to his critics, arguing that the status quo of family relations was not working very well. The traditional pattern "by which a woman is subdued, first to her father, and then to a husband of his choice is not in our present phase of civilisation working very satisfactorily. . . . I believe that the development of civilisation demands a revision of the constitution of the family and of our conventions of the relations of men and women, which will give the natural instincts of womanhood freer play. . . . The family *does not work* as it used to do, and we do not know why, and we have to look into it . . . so I enter my plea for an arrest of judgment and liberty of discussion in this vitally important field."

Once again Wells was ahead of his time. If he understood in advance that the airplane was going to change the nature of warfare, he was equally prescient in his nontechnical speculations. The status of women was changing, and with that change would come changes in the nature of the family, in the nature of accepted morality. Wells had violated the standards of morality, first by running away with Jane; now he had fathered a child out of wedlock and was recommending fundamental study and restructuring of the estate of marriage itself. He was riding the edge of change.

The controversy over *Ann Veronica* and the liberated ideas it contained helped Wells rather than hurt him. Within two years "many people were beginning to be ashamed of the violence of their reactions to *Ann Veronica* and others were plainly bored by the demands of my more persistent antagonists. . . . Instead of being made an outcast, finally and conclusively, I was made a sort of champion."

Nor were sales hurt by the controversy. "It sold and went on selling in a variety of editions." Wells's revolutionary approach to love and family had a wider effect: "After *Ann Veronica,* things were never quite the same again in the world of popular English fiction." Within a few years other writers would publish novels that followed Wells's and *Ann Veronica*'s lead. Writers such as D. H. Lawrence and James Joyce would make much of the increasing freedom to explore in fiction all aspects of morality—freedom that at least in part could be traced to Wells's boldness.

Wells himself had found a form in which to exert his influence. In *Ann Veronica* he examined a single question—love—and presented a new view of the subject. People paid attention. They may have been shocked, but he had their attention. The novel, then, as argument, as presentation of an idea or ideas, examination of ideas, discussion and amplification of ideas—this was the direction in which Wells would take his fiction. It would mean a farewell to any hopes of satisfying Henry James's aesthetic demands; there was little room in the artistic novel for anything so unaesthetic as discussion and debate of ideas. Wells had wanted to achieve a great artistic success, but he was drawn by his own nature in another direction.

Before undertaking another major novel, though, Wells wrote *The History of Mr. Polly,* a delightfully comic novel of a man's escape from a domineering wife. The central character of this novel, which appeared in 1910, seems to be a tribute to Joseph Wells, who died the same year.

If *Ann Veronica* had been a look at the rationale behind Wells's affair with Amber Reeves, *The New Machiavelli* was a look at the affair itself. This novel, published in 1911, dealt bluntly with the Fabians, with a man's attempt to escape from an unhappy marriage, with politics and crises both external and internal. In his hero, Remington, Wells portrayed a man not unlike himself.

Later Wells would look back at the story and see how much truth it held for himself. While writing the book he was seeking "a release completed in imagination if not in fact. I realize now . . . that the idea of going off somewhere—to Italy in the story—out of the tangle of Fabian disputes, tiresomely half-relevant politics and the routines of literary life, very nearly overwhelmed me in my own proper person, and the story of Remington . . . is essentially a dramatized wish."

Wells's dramatization of his problems was greeted with dismay by his publishers, who refused *The New Machiavelli*, feeling it to be as provocative and unprintable as *Ann Veronica*. *The New Machiavelli* was finally published by a small and less than respectable publisher, placing Wells in the position of being a distinguished writer whose latest novel was lumped with books deliberately scandalous.

While his professional life was causing him trouble, Wells's personal turmoil was beginning to subside. With Amber Reeves he had made his attempt to escape, and he had returned. His marriage with Jane was unusual, in many ways difficult for both of them, but at the same time they fulfilled certain needs for each other. On the surface theirs was a happy marriage.

Wells enjoyed many aspects of the successful writer's life. Spade House was filled with fun and games. There were frequent parties, and Jane was an ideal hostess, Wells a congenial and energetic host. He had a great love of games and was constantly exhorting his guests and family to indulge in rowdy sports and amusing parlor activities.

As his sons grew older Wells took special pleasure in devising entertainments for them. He was always ready to answer their questions, show them the wonders of books and ideas, discuss with them the problems and objects of curiosity which he, as a boy, had had to examine on his own. Such solitary questioning would not be forced upon Gip and Frank.

One of the favorite pastimes in the Wells household was an elaborate war game that Wells developed. A battlefield was created by spreading a variety of debris—bricks and rocks, bits of wood and boxes—across a large floor. Then sizable tin soldiers and animals were arrayed in ranks as opposing armies. Using small brass cannon that fired projectiles, the generals—Wells and his sons, or Wells and his guests—would take aim and fire. These small wars often lasted throughout the day, with breaks for regrouping, peace negotiations, stockpiling of weaponry.

Even in his mid-forties Wells retained his childish delight in battlefields and soldiers' finery. He wrote a book about his war games, *Little Wars*, published in 1913. This small volume communicates quite clearly Wells's enjoyment of his battles, the pleasure he took in being commanding officer of an armed force.

But they were just games, and by 1913 Wells began to tire of them. More than that, he came to see war games as vicious, even reprehensible. There was too much at stake in the real world, and those stakes were too often controlled by people who had never outgrown their war "games."

The world was changing—still!—and Wells's war games, for all the delight they brought him and his sons, were soon to be things of the past. Wells had said in his books that modern problems were rooted in old ways, and that to remain old-fashioned was to invite doom. Now doom loomed on the very near horizon, and Wells saw its sources even in the spread of toy soldiers and cannon across an imaginary battlefield.

War was so childish, and yet so inevitable. Wells's fascination with war had lingered since his own childhood, but by the second decade of the twentieth century he felt that it had lingered long enough. "For many years," he wrote, "my life was haunted by the fading memories of . . . early war fantasies. Up to 1914, I found a lively interest in playing a war game, with toy soldiers and guns. . . . I like to think I grew up out of that stage somewhen between 1916 and 1920 and began to think about war as a responsible adult should."

The time was arriving to put away the war games. And to put away much of the other paraphernalia of his life. He had come so far, but he still had far to go.

Spade House remained a delight, but perhaps he had lived there long enough. He'd written a great many books there, and from the study orchestrated his bid to transform the Fabian Society into his Order of Samurai. In Spade House he had transformed himself from a writer of popular scientific romances into a major thinker, a writer of popular serious and controversial novels. He'd fled Spade House for his love of Amber Reeves, and returned out of love and devotion to Jane and the children. In Spade House Wells grew up.

But it was time for a change. The boys were older. Wells and Jane understood each other. He put Spade House up for sale and moved his family back to London. He needed to be closer to the center of things. His dark vision of the future bore every promise of coming true, and if darkness were to be the destiny of mankind, then H. G. Wells was determined once more to be close to the heart of it.

There was war on the horizon and Wells knew that he could not stop its arrival. But he could do what he was able to see that this was the last time war would erupt and threaten the future of the world.

FIFTEEN

THE WAR THAT WILL END WAR

IN LONDON WELLS WENT on about his work. He could not liberate himself from his fears about the darkening of the world's destiny, but he was too disciplined to allow those fears to immobilize him. Although in London Wells found that much of his time was devoured by social demands—requests for lectures, solicitations of his support for various social and political causes, dozens of invitations to literary parties and functions—he still managed to put in long hours at his desk in his new study. Through all the distractions, the flow of material from his pen continued undiminished.

The first novel completed after leaving Spade House was another of his long novels of ideas. This one was called *Marriage,* and the focus of its ideas is revealed in its title.

Once more the novel served Wells as a convenient vehicle for presenting his ideas and arguments. In this case the arguments dealt with the nature of marriage and, as always in Wells's books, with the responsibilities of the superior person to the world in which he or she lived.

Marriage was not well received. On artistic grounds the book was criticized for being little more than a poorly dramatized lecture. On political grounds several feminists attacked Wells for not going far enough toward creating a fully independent and free-thinking woman character. One of the feminists who reacted most strongly to *Marriage* was a nineteen-year-old writer named Rebecca West. Born Cicily Fairfield, Rebecca West had, under her pseudonym, already established herself as an acute political commentator and writer. Her review of *Marriage* impressed Wells and he arranged a meeting.

The affair with Amber Reeves had faded into the past. Wells knew that he would not leave Jane, but at the same time he had come to an understanding of his own passions. He continued to search for the ideal woman, for the woman who fit his conception of the ideal—a combination of sharpness of intellect and keenness of physical desire and response. In Rebecca West, Wells saw a young woman who came closer than any other to embodying his ideals. Not least of her attractions was her ferocious sense of independence. Wells and Rebecca were attracted to each other and were soon enmeshed in a love affair.

This affair was different from Wells's previous attachment to Amber Reeves. Wells wanted no escape now. He had too much on his mind. No matter how deeply he threw himself into his work or play or romances, no matter how preoccupied he became with some new concern, he could not forget that the world in which he lived, the very world that just years earlier he had hoped to reshape into a modern utopia, was now spinning madly out of control. Great fortunes were being made in the manufacture and sale of weapons and armaments. Huge armies marched, huge navies sailed. Those were the realities of the world in the second decade of the twentieth century, and those were the catalysts that drove Wells's fears.

H. G. Wells, his mind already occupied with his writing, the state of the world, the prospects for war, his marriage, his relationship with Rebecca West, still found time to burden himself with another concern: his new home. As much as he enjoyed London, he came to understand that the great city could serve him better as a place occasionally visited rather than as a permanent home. After casting about for a more tranquil location for a home, he settled upon a former rectory in Essex.

Of course the home did not stay in its original state for long. Handsome and comfortable, the rectory nevertheless was the product of someone else's design and imagination. Wells had plenty of ideas concerning the proper nature of housing. He moved into the rectory in 1911, but by 1913 the tranquility was disrupted with the sounds of carpenters' hammers. Once the details of renovation were arranged, Wells left their implementation to Jane, while he returned to London and Rebecca.

Jane Wells accepted the demanding and emotionally trying conditions of her marriage with grace and dignity. She understood that her husband was an exceptional man, with exceptional ideas and needs. Her own sense of purpose and identity was fulfilled in the variety of ways in which she served H. G. Wells, not only as wife and mother, but also as hostess, business manager, typist, confidante, critic, and, most important, as the stable center of his increasingly hectic life. He could always return to Jane. Theirs had been a tumultuous relationship from the first, when they had lived together before Wells's divorce from Isabel was finalized. As the years passed, their relationship grew more stable, although the circumstances surrounding Wells's affairs made it seem chaotic to observers.

Wells was rarely in Essex. Even after the renovations of the home called Easton Glebe were completed—the house had a dozen bedrooms and was quite a showplace—Wells was on the move. In early 1914 he visited Russia for the first time. He was intrigued by the country and by the revolutionary attitudes he encountered among intellectuals there. His fascination, though, was to be interrupted on his return to England. Rebecca West was pregnant.

Rebecca's pregnancy did not keep Wells from his desk, although the scandal surrounding the child seriously interrupted Rebecca's career. Wells continued to write, in Essex with Jane, in London with Rebecca, and his work grew increasingly concerned with topical political questions and themes. The need for a world government was more pressing than ever, and Wells was doing everything he could to make people aware of that need.

In 1914 he had spelled out as clearly as he ever had the perils that awaited the world if a major war broke out. In *The World Set Free* Wells returned to prediction, foreseeing a period of complete global conflict, fought with overwhelmingly deadly weapons, a world war that destroys every government and social order on earth.

But there was a note of hope in *The World Set Free*. Wells had arrived at the conclusion that neither the gradual persuasion of the Fabians nor the revolution of the communists would be enough to clear the stage for the next and necessary act in civilization's evolution. Only the tragedy of war and the obliteration it brought would be sufficient to prepare the world for a single government.

Simultaneously with *The World Set Free*, Wells was at work on a series of articles that dealt with the dangers of warfare in the modern world. In these pieces Wells accurately forecast that the very technology that had made modern life so comfortable would, when turned to destruction, be more dreadful than anyone could imagine. In *The World Set Free* he postulated an awesomely destructive weapon: a bomb that derived its destructive force from the atom itself.

The world state, he argued, was the only way for the salvation of mankind to be accomplished.

It was not to be. Everything Wells had written, every pronouncement he made, was an attempt to make people see that the way they lived and the way they ran their nations and their world were ways that would doom them to repeat, on ever larger and more terrifying scales, the catastrophes that had always plagued humanity. Times changed, details changed, technology changed, but human nature remained tragically the same.

As his sons became young men, as new life grew within Rebecca West, the world's tragic nature manifested itself. On June 28, 1914, Francis Ferdinand, archduke of Austria, was assassinated. With his death the stage was set for World War I.

Rebecca's child was born on August 4, 1914. It was a boy who was named Anthony West. On the same day Great Britain declared war on Germany. Wells's mind was doubly occupied: an announcement of a birth, a declaration that could only mean hundreds of thousands of deaths. The parallel was too ironic. That night he sat at his desk and wrote furiously. His thoughts raced ahead; he was virtually flinging words onto paper. He wrote of the conflict ahead, reminding his countrymen that they were fighting not only to crush the Germans and to guarantee their own liberty; they were also fighting for the future—the future of their children and their nation, the future of the world and all the world's children.

In the title of the pamphlet he wrote during that long August night, Wells summed up his feelings and hopes about the First World War. In its title he coined a phrase that would echo throughout the conflict and beyond it, a phrase still known today. The pamphlet was called *The War That Will End War*.

Whether or not the war actually would put an end to armed conflict remained to be seen. It quickly became clear, though, that the war would not end soon. New weapons wreaked carnage on an almost unimaginable scale, but both sides found themselves before long in a stalemate, their battle lines drawn, their positions fortified. The only movement came when one side would rise out of its trenches for a futile attack against the enemy. And after they had been battered and repulsed they would wait in the mud for the enemy to waste its own men in an equally futile assault.

Wells had seen so much of it coming. Years had passed since the publication of *The War in the Air*. Now aircraft soared through the skies, their pilots using newly perfected machine guns to shoot one another down.

Aircraft were not the only weapons Wells had foreseen. In a short story called "The Land Ironclads," published in 1903, Wells wrote with almost astonishing accuracy of great mechanical war engines: tanks. Now, in Europe, tanks were being used in actuality. Like many prophets Wells wished his vision had been less keen.

Still, the war was upon the world and Wells threw himself and all of his energy into doing what he could to help end it. He became quite a patriot, insisting in violent arguments with George Bernard Shaw, among others, that there was no use wasting time trying to analyze the nature of the war as the Fabians were doing. There was only time to get on with the business of winning it. The Germans, Wells insisted, must be crushed absolutely. Wells called for all who loved freedom to rally to the cause. He saw the war as the last stand for civilization.

Shaw and the Fabians were not the only ones with whom Wells was in conflict. His old friend Henry James had published, shortly before the outbreak of the war, a pair of literary essays that gently indicted Wells, among others, for being less than fully committed to the cause of art. In haste and annoyance, and to take his mind off the war, Wells put together a response.

The response took the form of a novel, *Boon,* in the form of a series of articles written by "George Boon." In one of the articles Wells made fun of James's mannerisms, his fastidious artistry. There was an element of cruelty in *Boon,* and it brought the friendship between Wells and James to a melancholy close. It was all the more ironic, for James's belief in the rightness of the Allied cause was equal to Wells's; James, in fact, gave up his American citizenship when the United

States refused to enter the war. Henry James died in 1916, the year after the publication of *Boon*.

The literary conflict with James was ill-considered, but Wells wasted little time on it. As much as he could, he ignored the controversy surrounding *Boon* and applied himself to journalism, filling newspapers and magazine columns with hastily composed articles and letters exhorting his fellow Britons to victory over the Germans. It struck Wells that this war was nothing less than the conflict he'd anticipated—the battle between the old order (Germany) and the new order (the Allies). The new order must win.

Wells held firm to this attitude throughout the first two years of the war. Then a strange thing happened. After all of his efforts to inspire in his countrymen a sense of the importance and rightness of the Allied cause, Wells had a revelation.

It was 1916. Wells was walking down a London street, on his way to lunch, his mind filled with a variety of thoughts. .He was searching for ways to do more toward speeding an Allied victory.

Then he was distracted by a large poster. He stopped to read it, noticing that it was a royal proclamation, a public message from King George V. As Wells stood on that London corner reading the proclamation, he felt as though he had been blind and could at last see. In the words of the proclamation lay the truth about the First World War, and nothing H. G. Wells could do would change that truth.

In the words of the poster the king called for great effort on the part of "my people." Wells understood. It was as it had always been throughout history: a leader demanding sacrifice from his subjects, a leader placing himself above them.

Wells stood there for a few moments, then walked on. His mind was still busy, but was busy now digesting this new understanding. Nothing changed.

He would write later of that poster and the thoughts it inspired in him. "So long as you suffer any man to call himself your shepherd sooner or later you will find yourself with a crook around your ankle." And even more bitterly: "We are not making war against Germany; we were being ordered about in the King's war with Germany."

Neither side represented a new order; neither side was more virtuous than the other. This war was simply one more war, the modernized descendant of every war since humans first fought against one another. History was filled with such conflicts and confrontations, and none of them had ever solved anything more than temporarily. History was a vast and bloody tapestry, and that afternoon and for the rest of the war all of history rested upon Wells's shoulders.

He forced himself to push history to the back of his mind, at least for the time being. There would be time to deal with history later. For now, there were young men dying in the mud of Europe, and there ought to be something H. G. Wells could do for them.

He visited the front. He saw the conditions under which soldiers lived and fought and died. One of the problems that most severely affected the soldiers was their inability to move supplies and wounded through the mire. There was a limit to how much a man could carry. The difficulties caused by the mud, along with the need for an efficient and effective means of transporting supplies, stayed in Wells's mind.

Then one night he sat upright in his bed. He was back in England but he could not free himself from thoughts of soldiers struggling and exhausting themselves in the muddy trenches. Men even died in the mud, drowning as though in quicksand. At home, safe in the warmth and comfort of his bed, Wells's busy brain had come up with a solution.

He stayed up all night, making notes and sketches. What he had devised was called a "mobile telepherage system." It consisted of a series of vertical poles with crossbars, large T's. These T-shaped poles could be raised and lowered easily. Between the crossbars would be strung wires, and the wires would be driven by an engine. Supplies, ammunition, even wounded soldiers could be carried on the wires, much as skiers ride on ski lifts. The system would be portable, virtually invisible from the air, easily repaired. It would save thousands of lives.

Wells set to work immediately to have his "telepherage" system developed and implemented. He met with Winston Churchill, then involved with Britain's Ministry of Munitions. Churchill saw to it that some research was done and some systems developed. But it was one more project that got lost in the bureaucratic maze of the government. And when a few of the systems were actually delivered to the front they proved to be too little, too late.

The war dragged on. Casualties were now measured in millions. Wells, having lost patience with the governmental mind, soon found himself equally disgusted by the military mind. Wells had outgrown his love of war games; men such as Churchill never did. They remained, Wells was convinced, little boys playing with their toy soldiers. Only now their toys were living, breathing, bleeding, dying young men—who just a few years earlier had been children.

It was from thoughts of such young men, and thoughts of his own sons and of Anthony West, now two, that Wells derived his greatest contribution to the war effort. That contribution was, as might be expected, not an invention but a book.

It was a novel, the finest he had written in years. It was called *Mr. Britling Sees It Through.*

Mr. Britling is a famous English writer; he is, in fact, a very thinly disguised H. G. Wells. In the opening chapters of the book Mr. Britling is visited by a brash young American who admires his work. The American spends some time with the Britlings, and sees the happy life the author has made for himself. There is a fine country home, good food and conversation, many games. There is a young German tutor, a young man devoted to Britling's sons. Everything is happy, there is a sense of well-being and hope.

But war comes, and happiness vanishes. The tutor, loved by his charges, returns to his homeland to battle against the nation of his friends. Britling's eldest son enlists in the army. The young American is torn by his country's neutrality. Mr. Britling stays up all night writing essays about war.

The final chapters of *Mr. Britling Sees It Through* are as emotionally harrowing as any Wells ever wrote. The story moves toward its conclusion inexorably: Nothing good can ever come of war. Or at least no good can ever be achieved upon a field of battle. The results of one battle, one war, are simply to draw the lines for the next battle, and establish allies for the next war.

Britling, at the novel's conclusion, sees this clearly. He composes a letter to the parents of the German tutor, killed in the war as had been Britling's son Hugh. In the letter Mr. Britling seeks answers to vital questions:

"What have we been fighting for? . . . Do you know? Does any one know? . . . Why should we be puppets any longer in the hands of crowned fools and witless diplomats? Even if we were dumb and acquiescent before, does not the blood of our sons now cry out to us that this foolery should cease? We have let these people send our sons to death.

"It is you and I who must stop these wars, these massacres of boys. . . .

"Let us set ourselves with all our minds and all our hearts to the perfecting and working out of the methods of democracy and the ending for ever of the kings and emperors and priestcrafts and the bands of adventurers, the traders and owners and forestallers who have betrayed mankind into this morass of hate and blood—in which our sons are lost—in which we flounder still. . . ."

As he writes the long letter Mr. Britling, for the first time, has a vision of God—not the traditional god of churches and "priestcrafts," but his own vision of God, a God in whom Hugh and the German tutor, in whom all the young men killed in the war, are embodied. This was a new God, ". . . the Master, the Captain of Mankind . . . God, the Captain of the World Republic . . ."

Mr. Britling—and H. G. Wells—arrive at the end of the novel with something like a holy crusade on their minds. To continue sacrificing the world's greatest treasure—its young—for the preservation of meaningless national boundaries was absurd, Wells wrote. What must be called for was a war for one goal and one goal only. Not a war that will end war: Wells had seen all too clearly how sentimentally optimistic that idea was. Rather, a war fought by a united effort of caring and responsible nations to eradicate the armed forces of any nation that would rise up against another. A war *against* war.

As the carnage of the First World War drew to a close Wells found that he had touched a nerve. *Mr. Brittling Sees It Through* was his biggest success in years. The public responded eagerly and emotionally to Mr. Britling's promise that the deaths of millions of young men not be in vain. The novel became an instant best-seller in England. The reaction in the United States was equally enthusiastic. In Russia, severely battered by the war, *Mr. Britling* was hailed as the most vivid and moving account yet of the tragedy of World War I.

Meanwhile Wells was striving to make Mr. Britling's ideals a reality. He was fired up once more with his boundless enthusiasm for world government. The difference was that this time, perhaps for the first time, there seemed to be a possibility of that goal actually being realized.

H. G. Wells was not alone in seeing global order as a goal of global conflict. During the war a variety of influential people began to call for some sort of world government. Their objective, first announced during the opening weeks of the conflict, was the formation of a "League of Nations."

It was not until 1916 that Wells became involved with

the plans for this League, but when he did it was with all of his enthusiasm, as well as with all of his determination to have things his way. He immediately rephrased the name of the organization, calling for a "League of *Free* Nations." He felt it important that all member nations be republics, nations ruled by the people. Wells remained convinced that world government could only be developed after the abolition of monarchies and dictatorships. For the whole world to be a republic, each of its individual nations must first become republics.

The greatest weapon Wells had in the battle for the establishment of the League was, of course, his pen, and he put it to good use. Articles, letters, and pamphlets appeared with almost astonishing frequency. For a time it seemed that he was determined to fill every newspaper and magazine with his thoughts, with his demands for a new world order.

In 1918 Wells assembled his pieces in a book called *In the Fourth Year*. In this book he clearly set forth his vision of the sort of changes and sacrifices that must be made should the world government hope to succeed. *In the Fourth Year* held detailed prescriptions for the formation of the world government. Every nation must surrender its armed forces, must establish a government by republic, must be willing to follow the rules established by the central League. Any nation that transgressed against the League would face the armies of the League itself. War *against* war.

It was a fine plan. As always with Wells, he became immediately convinced that his plan would be adopted, and that at last a permanent peace—or at least a force empowered to fight for such a peace—was on the horizon. He did not rest his pen, writing not only books and articles, but also letters to leaders, including President Woodrow Wilson. It was imperative, Wells insisted, that the treaties that ended the First World War be designed and negotiated in such a way as to form the groundwork for an effective League of Free Nations.

Once again, though, Wells neglected to take into account the nature of the world. He expected the leaders to listen to him and his colleagues and then proceed to put their ideas to work. Governments were charged, after all, with enacting the most sensible and hopeful programs for their people; what programs could be more sensible than those H. G. Wells and the other intellectuals of the age had developed?

It was not to be. Wells watched with great anger and dismay as the war ended and the negotiations and formation of a League of Nations proceeded. The leaders of government were no more concerned with a just and lasting peace than were children when they played war games. The leaders were interested in preserving their power, in holding onto trade agreements, in serving their own limited interests.

When, in 1920, the League of Nations was actually formed it fell far short of the grand organization Wells and others had envisioned. It had no armed forces. It had few means of enforcing its regulations. In reality, the League of Nations was a gesture, a promising but virtually empty symbol. The United States did not even belong to the League, nor, except for a brief period, did the newly formed Union of Soviet Socialist Republics.

Over the next twenty-six years the impotence of the League as a peace-keeping organization would be demonstrated again and again. While it did help settle conflicts in South America and the Balkans, it stood helpless as Japan invaded Manchuria, as the USSR attacked Finland in 1939, as the forces of the Second World War built and erupted.

Wells could only shake his head bitterly. Once again he'd allowed his hopes to soar in defiance of what he knew was true about human nature. Looking back he would state that the glorious future was "in the hands of men of limited outlooks and small motives, whose chief control was their servitude to tradition. . . . Men of my way of thinking were left helpless, voiceless and altogether baffled. . . . What seemed to be the portal of a World Control standing wide open to us, was shut and slammed in our faces."

Servitude to tradition. It was the old argument, the old enemy that had haunted Wells from his days as a student. The present was dominated by the past, and that domination doomed the future. And no one seemed to understand the past that held such sway over them. Not until people truly understood the nature of their history could they begin to rise above it. But how could they be made to understand that history? Wells had an idea, a bold idea.

With the future once more darkening before him, Wells turned his attention to the past.

SIXTEEN

EDUCATION OR CATASTROPHE?

THE POSSIBILITY OF AN effective League of Free Nations had collapsed, it seemed to Wells, because people were not yet ready for it. His new task was to make them ready. He returned to one of his earliest and most consistently held articles of faith: The nature of society would not change for the better until the nature of the individuals who made up society was changed.

One of the most disturbing things he had noticed during the League of Nations fiasco was that virtually every member of the committees and groups who worked on the plans for the League possessed differing and sometimes wildly divergent ideas about the world and its history. Not only would the committee members argue over the details of the League's charter, they also fought over historical matters. But history was supposedly a collection of "facts." How could there be such serious disagreement over the nature of history? And more important, how could those disagreements be settled? Wells believed that not until people had a solid and accurate grounding in the history of their world could they make intelligent plans for its future.

He grew more and more concerned that the general public be taught something of world history before memories of history's latest and bloodiest upheaval faded. The message must be spread. Even as Wells served on committees planning the League he was arguing that one of the organization's primary functions must be to improve education throughout the world. In a pamphlet published in 1919, *History Is One,* Wells proposed that such a world history should show the growth of the world toward a central, single government. Such a presentation of history was vital for the prevention of future wars.

Pamphlets were not enough. What was called for was a serious and ambitious world history. In essence what Wells sought was a gathering of historical knowledge into a single book, a compendium of history, which, by showing where the world had been, would point the way toward where the world was going.

It was Wells's hope and intention to persuade distinguished historians to work together on this world history. He learned quickly that such hopes were futile. The world of universities was still a part of the larger world, and the attitudes of historians in those universities were not too different from the attitudes Wells had encountered when working for the League. The historians argued among themselves over details and were unwilling to compromise in order to present a large picture. They were not interested in large ideas, only in their own little corners of knowledge. The prospect of examining history as a whole did not attract them.

Wells soon realized he would have to take the task upon himself. He was no professional historian, but history had been a particular passion since the days recuperating on the couch in Atlas House. He was no scholar, but that might prove to be an advantage. Wells would be free from the jealous protection of reputation and respect that afflicted many university-bound scholars. Wells could concentrate upon making history clear to average readers, rather than worrying about what historians thought.

Before beginning the history he gave the project a great

deal of serious thought. The more he thought, the more important this work of history became to him. He and Jane passed several hours discussing the wisdom of his applying himself to so ambitious an undertaking. It would take at least a year of his life, and possibly more, in order to do properly. There seemed little chance that this history of the world would make much money. Wells studied his finances carefully: He not only had his family in Easton Glebe to care for, there were also Rebecca and Anthony West. But *Mr. Britling*'s success had left his bank balance healthy. If he was not truly rich, he was at least very comfortable. He could safely undertake his history without risking his responsibilities.

There was more than financial risk at stake. Wells knew that he was risking his career as a serious novelist. Since *Mr. Britling Sees It Through* he had published some fiction. There had been another long novel, *Joan and Peter,* on the subject of education. There had been other novels. But to surrender novel writing for a year or more, and at the end of that time deliver a work of history to the public—what would happen to his reputation as a novelist?

It was a serious question, but it had been answered long before Wells undertook his history. Wells himself would later realize that *Mr. Britling* was his last truly popular novel. He was moving on a steady course in his own direction now, setting his own pace and making his own demands upon his readers, leaving the large popular audiences and critical acclaim to newer novelists who were breaking ground of their own. The time belonged to writers such as D. H. Lawrence, and in America F. Scott Fitzgerald and, soon, Ernest Hemingway. Wells's approach to the novel suddenly seemed dated, a relic existing beyond its time.

New writers such as Virginia Woolf, James Joyce, and Marcel Proust were revolutionizing the form and nature of the novel. Wells had little use for them. He had worked hard to break new ground himself, to use the novel as a popular forum for presenting and discussing bold ideas. This new generation of novelists was more concerned with using the novel personally, presenting individual ideas and impressions, generally ignoring the blatant philosophizing that had become Wells's trademark.

Virginia Woolf, whose stream of consciousness explorations of her characters' psychological natures attracted great attention and influenced an entire generation of novelists, summed up what she—and by implication many of her generation—felt was wrong with Wells's fictional methods. She postulated a woman in a carriage. H. G. Wells, she said, would be more concerned with the woman's rent, with the conditions that made her rent so high, with the nature of housing, than he would with the nature of the woman's mental state.

No matter. Art had always preoccupied Wells, but when the time came to put words on paper, art had always placed second to *idea*. Henry James, Joseph Conrad, Virginia Woolf —Wells was an easy target for more self-conscious artists. Now he was gearing up to deal with ideas more directly than ever before, without worrying about characters or plot. He would forget novels for a while. He had earned a rest and his laurels were not so shabby. There were a score of first-rate novels with the name H. G. Wells upon the spine.

Now, though, history gave him a plot and story more broad than anything even he could conjure out of imagination. All of history was his to write about. As he wrote he did not allow himself to forget how important this new cause was. Although he did not expect to sell many copies of his history, he did hope that it would have an effect on the way history was taught. Public education satisfied Wells no more in the twentieth century than it had in the nineteenth. The purpose of education, it seemed to Wells, remained the passing on to children of the prejudices and ignorances that had ruined their parents' world. Poor education played as large a part in the continuing cycle of destruction as did guns and armies. Wells hoped that in some way his book of history would help to change that.

He put his purpose in a single chilling phrase. "Human history," he wrote, "becomes more and more a race between education and catastrophe."

With that thought in mind, and convinced of his own high purpose, Wells worked as hard as he had ever worked in his life. The scope of the project would have daunted even the most ambitious writers, but Wells was not deterred. He spent long hours hunched over his desk, writing thousands of words each day. Around him stood his reference books, open to various chapters from which he gleaned the raw facts of history. Wells's pen raced across page after page, propelled by his energy and enthusiasm, transforming those raw facts into a coherent and compelling outline of history.

Wells's working methods during the composition of *The Outline of History* reveal that while he was not concerned with losing himself in pointless academic arguments over minor questions, he nonetheless took great pains to ensure historical accuracy. He inquired of distinguished scholars for assistance in planning his research and guiding his reading. He worked closely with the book's illustrator, J. F. Horrabin, and was delighted with the many fine maps and pictures that accompanied his text.

During the actual writing of the book, Wells followed a schedule that helped contribute to overall accuracy. He would draft a section of the book, then circulate copies of that section among his advisers. They would criticize the work and make corrections. When the corrected pages were returned, Wells worte them once more, eliminating errors and incorporating some of the suggestions. It was exhausting work but also exhilarating.

The book grew and grew, outstripping even Wells's mighty ambitions. He worked on it for more than a full year. Including later revisions and alterations, *The Outline of*

History took nearly three years to complete. But when the book was finished few would argue that the investment had not been worthwhile.

The Outline of History is a remarkable achievement. It towered over other popular histories of its day, establishing by its thoroughness and vigor a standard that is still felt today. This was history freed, as much as was possible, from narrowness and nationalism. Wells told the story of history as the story of a *world*. He saw the whole picture and that was the picture he sought to pass on to his readers.

He began before the dawn of history, before, even, the dawn of life. The early sections of the book hold reminders of Wells's lifelong study of evolution. The reader sees, as Wells did, the beauty of the development of each new organism.

Wells's sure hand guides the story through man's appearance and evolution, the rise of villages, the triumphs and tragedies of early civilizations, war and more war. It was a beautiful and awesome performance. Wells's powers were at their peak.

History was brought to compelling life for nonacademic readers. That was Wells's greatest achievement in *The Outline of History*, and it was the achievement he hoped most to accomplish. He wanted to make history accessible to the average reader, to people who wished to learn history but who could not work their way through the turgid and difficult prose affected by professors of history. In addition, Wells wanted his book to be free of what he called "King and Country stuff," and at that he also succeeded.

His great risk paid off in terms of the book's scope, content, and execution, and Wells was astonished and pleased to find *The Outline of History* a financial success as well. The book first appeared in twenty-five separate and self-contained installments, each telling part of the story, each selling out 100,000-copy printings as soon as they appeared. When the book version was released in 1920, it was an even larger success. Wells's publishers, both in England and the United States, had held some doubts about the *Outline*'s commercial prospects, just as Wells himself had. Wells derived considerable amusement from the fact that this book of questionable prospects sold more than *two million* copies in its first few years in print. Its success made him wealthier than ever before and freed him from any further concerns about money.

He wished that *The Outline of History*'s success could free him from his other concerns, particularly his concerns about the future of the human race. The dilemma of education versus catastrophe weighed heavily upon him, and he hoped that his contribution to the understanding of history would be put to work in the schools. It was a book, Wells felt, that might help tilt the scales away from catastrophe.

His hopes went unrealized. While the general public loved the book, most professional historians did not. Wells had invaded their territory. They were quick to seize upon any small error in the text and to use those errors to cast doubt upon the whole undertaking. Small errors were unavoidable in a book almost three-quarters of a million words long. The critics did not acknowledge that Wells was scrupulous about correcting any errors that were pointed out. *The Outline of History* would go through several revisions during Wells's lifetime, and each would serve to make an already accurate book even more accurate. But Wells's painstaking attention and concern meant little to the scholars. *The Outline of History* was not taught in schools.

Later Wells would write that it remained "a matter of luck whether or no an intelligent boy or girl ever comes to the newer rendering of historical fact." The schools were content to begin the study of history with, in England the medieval period, in America the Revolutionary War or perhaps the Pilgrims. Such "King and Country stuff" crippled the minds of students, left them unaware of the great flow of history from man's early evolution to the world state that lay just beyond the horizon. But the schools would not listen to H. G. Wells.

Neither would he listen to them. He continued to formulate his own theories of education. He gave the subject some of the most serious and extended thought of his career. He reached some conclusions about the best ways to prepare students for the challenges of a difficult world. "I am convinced," he wrote, "that the . . . framework of a proper education should be presented as . . . the three sides of the triangle . . . Biology, History and Human Ecology. A child should begin with Natural History, a History of Inventions, Social Beginnings and Descriptive Geography, that should constitute its first world picture, and the treatment of these subjects should broaden and intensify before specialization."

He went on, this tireless worker for a better world, to tell what he thought such an education would accomplish. "I believe that minds resting on that triple foundation will be equipped for the role of world citizens, and I do not believe that a world community can be held together in a common understanding except upon such a foundation."

The Outline of History cemented H.G. Wells's reputation as one of the leading thinkers of his time. He towered above other writers and thinkers just as his *Outline* towered above other histories. The reading public might be looking to others for fashionable novels, but they turned to H. G. Wells for guidance in forming opinions about the past, the present, and the future.

As always, Wells obliged. He was forever in the forefront of intellectual trend setters, continually calling the public's attention to matters that might otherwise have passed unconsidered.

In 1920 Wells became one of the first writers of international stature to visit Russia after the revolution in which communists seized control of the government. His trip to the newly formed Soviet Union was prompted by an invitation from Maxim Gorky, who wrote requesting Wells's aid in providing supplies for starving Russian scientists. Wells, accompanied by Gip, now a young man of nineteen, visited the Soviet Union in the fall of 1920.

While he met with many of the Russian leaders and scientists, it was his meeting with Vladimir Ilich Lenin, leader of the Bolsheviks, that most intrigued Wells. Lenin was a charismatic man, a visionary who was actually attempting to put his vision into action. Wells, of course, was impressed with Lenin, but, being Wells, felt it his responsibility to lecture the communist leader on the importance of a revolution in Soviet education as well as economy. Lenin was not impressed.

Still, Wells felt that he had learned a few things from his visit, and he put his thoughts into a book, *Russia in the Shadows*. In this book, as well as in other pieces written about Russia and its revolution, Wells sought to shift the course of public opinion about the new Russian leaders. He tried to persuade the British government to send aid to the Russians and to recognize the communists as the legitimate leaders of Russia.

Wells's persuasive powers were very great, but he was asking too much. Sentiment ran high against the Bolsheviks, and Wells soon found himself under attack in print. One of the most caustic and angry attacks came from Winston Churchill, long an opponent of the Bolsheviks and Lenin. Wells, perhaps too hastily, returned the attack by calling Churchill a variety of names in print and stating that Churchill was no statesman, merely an imitation of one and, further, that as government leaders went, Winston Churchill was little more than an infected sore, oozing waste throughout England.

The battle was joined. Letters flew left and right, with some of England's most notable political and literary leaders exchanging opinions about Wells, Churchill, Lenin, and the rest. Even Sidney Webb of the Fabians, Wells's old antagonist, found himself once more maligned in print.

Wells rode through the middle of the controversy, dashing off letters, defending his honor, clarifying his positions, trying to make people see that the Russians were neither villains nor saints, just people undertaking a new form of government. Wells did not endorse the Bolsheviks, but he did admire the attempt to arrive at a new way of shaping a nation.

The controversy and debate did not slow his pen. He was still hard at work on the *Outline,* refining it and making it even more available to the average reader through a condensation called *A Short History of the World.* In addition, his success with the *Outline* led him to envision an even more ambitious scheme for public education.

His discussions with Lenin—and Lenin's unwillingness to give serious attention to Wells's plan for Soviet education—reconfirmed Wells's conviction that it was only through a concerted and intelligent approach to education that the world could be saved. England had no such plan, nor did the Soviet Union, or the United States, or any nation on earth.

Wells, though, could not ignore the eagerness and enthusiasm with which the public responded to *The Outline of History.* People wanted to learn the truth; they were ready for a general reconstruction of education even if their educators were not. They needed only a leader who would guide them through the world of knowledge.

Who better to lead than H. G. Wells? He returned to his triad of disciplines: history, biology, economics. Suppose, he thought, *The Outline of History* were to become merely the first volume of a shelf of books, which, when completed, would offer any reader a solid grounding in the most important areas of human knowledge and endeavor. Such a series of books would be more than a set of references. Properly done, the books would serve as a sort of Bible of Civilization.

As these thoughts took shape, Wells had occasion to reflect upon one man who shared his vision of a universal education. This was F. W. Sanderson, a schoolmaster to whom Wells had entrusted his own sons as they reached school age. Like Wells, Sanderson felt that the purpose of education was to teach children to see the world as a whole, an attitude and outlook that greatly endeared him to Wells. Upon Sanderson's death Wells wrote a biography entitled *The Story of a Great Schoolmaster,* which not only paid tribute to Sanderson but also served to present, once more, Wells's vision of a proper universal education.

As the twenties unfolded, Wells became more committed to the idea of extending his shelf of *Outlines.* The idea was too important, the format too effective to leave with only a book of history. Other subjects could be brought under Wells's gaze and interpreted for the average reader. He began planning an outline of biology.

There were distractions that slowed the work. His relationship with Rebecca came to a close after ten years. She was beginning to reestablish her own career, and Wells's demands upon her became increasingly petulant, his attitude domineering. After they stopped seeing each other he continued to support their son, Anthony, and indeed introduced Anthony to Gip and Frank. Rebecca West would go on to become one of the most respected writers of the century, bringing her exceptional intelligence and great craft to both fiction and nonfiction over the course of a long career. Wells was bitter and angry about the end of the relationship—which was Rebecca's idea—and for years would not speak with her without harshness.

He also continued to write novels and accepted a great variety of journalistic assignments. Early in the twenties he ran for political office, including a seat in Parliament. Voters were willing to listen to Wells, were eager to read his books, but could not bring themselves to put him in office.

In 1924, at the age of fifty-eight, Wells found himself falling into a depression. He continued to plan and work at his outline of knowledge, but even that task could not hold his attention. His children were nearly adults. England had embraced his books but not his wisdom. The dreaded Churchill, and others like him, had achieved political power, perpetuating all the ills Wells loathed. The world pressed in on him. Rebecca abandoned him. He could not think clearly.

The wealth earned by *The Outline of History* gave Wells the freedom to do as he pleased. He took a leave of absence from England. He found a home in the south of France. He visited England and Jane occasionally. He tried to think things through.

His thinking yielded one of the longest novels of his career. *The World of William Clissold* occupied Wells's attention for nearly three years. He spent the time in France thinking carefully, going for long walks in the sun, shaping his message.

He had a new vision of the world state. Governments had failed to create it, had failed even to attempt it in a serious way. The League of Nations was already perceived as a failure. Education offered great hope for the future, but education was slow, and universal education a task that would take centuries to accomplish. Wells recalled his failure to convert existing organizations such as the Fabians or the Bolsheviks to his cause. What other path to world government could there be?

The path Wells found and elucidated in *The World of William Clissold* lay through international cooperation of business and industrial and scientific leaders. These leaders held the power to create a new world in the open, with their networks of contacts and mutual benefit, an Open Conspiracy, as Wells called it.

William Clissold, the novel's narrator, is an industrialist who retires to a country home in the south of France for the purpose of thinking through the state of the world and the ways in which he might help to improve that state. Clissold develops his idea of an Open Conspiracy to wrest control of the world's fate away from the politicians and soldiers.

Clissold's nature was so close to Wells's that Wells felt obliged to include in the novel a preface that stated that the book was not autobiographical. The preface was not convincing. In many ways Clissold was Wells, just as Mr. Britling had been.

The book aroused great controversy when it appeared in 1926. Wells called for his Open Conspiracy to be effected by an elite, over the protest of the masses. It was an argument Wells had presented before: The path to the world state must be mapped and paved by men and women of vision. The rest must follow.

In the wake of the controversy that accompanied the publication of *The World of William Clissold*, Wells gave a series of lectures in which he further defined his vision of the new world. Jane accompanied him to France when he addressed the Sorbonne. They returned to England in 1927 to enjoy Gip's wedding. After the wedding Wells set off again in search of solitude in which to plan the next volume of his Bible of Civilization.

He had not been gone long when he received a letter from his son Frank. The news was bad. Jane was dying of cancer.

Wells raced to his wife's side, and they passed the final few months of her life together. Jane's last wish was to live long enough to see Frank's wedding, set for October 7, 1927.

Her wish did not come true. Amy Catherine Wells, Jane, Wells's wife for more than three decades, the woman who shared his rise from struggling journalist to one of the world's most influential men, died on October 6, the day before Frank's wedding.

H. G. and Jane Wells had had an unusual marriage. She

in many ways had surrendered her individuality to his needs. Certainly she indulged his passions with more grace and understanding than most would be capable of. She understood from the first that her husband was not like other men, and that their marriage could not be like other marriages.

And now she was gone. H. G. Wells was sixty-one, and although there would be other women in his life, there would be no more marriages. He set to work immediately writing a touching memoir of Jane, *The Book of Amy Catherine Wells*, which contained some of her own writing.

When that short work was completed he turned his attention back to the future. His time on earth, he realized, was limited. In what time remained he wanted to drive home even more forcefully than before his dream of a united world, of an Open Conspiracy, a world of universal knowledge and peace. He had more work to do.

SEVENTEEN

THINGS TO COME

Wells threw himself even more completely into his work. The next volume of his Bible of Civilization was the first piece on his agenda. It would be called *The Science of Life,* and would provide for the average reader an introduction to the world of biology.

For this project Wells knew he would require more than proofreaders and consultants; he would need collaborators who could augment his vision with their own detailed knowledge of biology. Fortunately for Wells he knew two men who were perfect for the job. One of them was the distinguished biologist Julian Huxley, grandson of Wells's teacher Thomas Henry Huxley.

The other collaborator was even closer to Wells's heart. His name was George Philip Wells. Gip was now a scientist himself, a teacher of biology. Wells's early hope for his own career found fruition in the distinguished scientific career of his son.

The three labored hard on *The Science of Life.* Work on the huge book kept Wells busy through the closing years of the twenties. *The Science of Life* appeared in 1930, and although it sold well, it achieved nothing like the success of *The Outline of History.*

Wells paid little attention. Even as the closing pages of

The Science of Life were being written, Wells was working with other collaborators on his third outline, this one dealing with economics. Called *The Work, Wealth and Happiness of Mankind,* this volume did not do well at all. In part its failure may be attributed to Wells's lack of fellowship with his collaborators, in part to the difficulty of the subject: Economics did not lend itself easily to popularization.

And through it all Wells wrote articles and essays and novels. Even in his mid-sixties his energy was astonishing. He seemed always to have half a dozen projects going at once. Juggling so many disparate undertakings was an effort even for Wells, but he would not slow his pace. Perhaps he could not. He was too much aware of the catastrophe that lay ahead if his words were not heeded. Already he could sense the gathering clouds of yet another world war.

He put his fears into another novel of the future. This story was no scientific romance, but rather a scientific nightmare in which Wells told the story of the future as one of horrible and endless warfare, of the collapse of civilization, of the degradation of the human spirit. But out of the collapse comes a glimmer of hope, brought once more by one of Wells's elite groups, in this book the fliers whose aircraft had caused so much of the destruction in the first place. The book was called *The Shape of Things to Come: The Ultimate Revolution,* and it appeared in 1933.

Wells, living alone, his sons grown, could afford to travel where he pleased. In 1934 he decided to put that freedom to good use, visiting President Franklin Delano Roosevelt in the United States, and Josef Stalin, secretary of the Communist party and leader of the Soviet Union. The journeys to Washington and Moscow would be taxing for a man of Wells's years, but he wanted to see firsthand what these two leaders were doing to help shape the future.

An economic collapse and depression had enveloped the world. Both the United States and the Soviet Union faced serious challenges and great problems. Both nations were led by strong men whose visions broke sharply with the past. How willing, Wells wondered, were these two leaders to strive not only to overcome their present problems, but also to create a world state?

In Washington Wells found himself charmed by President Roosevelt. Wells felt almost as though he were meeting in person a leader of his own Open Conspiracy. He came away convinced that if FDR were not really an Open Conspirator, "he represents the way thither. . . . He is bold and unlimited in his objectives because his mental arms are long and his courage great. . . . Exactly what a modern government ought to be."

Later events would prompt Wells to temper somewhat his admiration for President Roosevelt, but in 1934 he felt that the United States, at least, possessed a leader who was doing what he could to set in motion something like the Open Conspiracy.

In July Wells and Gip set out for Russia to meet Stalin. From Berlin he and Gip flew to Moscow. The flight did not pass without Wells reflecting on how such a means of transportation had been laughed at when he wrote of it four decades before. Wells himself could laugh now, comfortable and safe in a modern aircraft.

The meeting with Stalin was less hopeful than the meeting with Roosevelt. Wells accurately perceived Stalin as more of a dictator than a leader who would unite his people. Wells was distressed at Stalin's unwillingness to listen to anything other than his own opinions. Stalin in person persuaded Wells to change his perceptions somewhat. During their conversations Wells came to see Stalin as a man too limited of vision to be an Open Conspirator, but nonetheless a leader who was getting on with the work of rebuilding his nation.

Still, the trip to Russia was as disheartening as the trip to the United States had been optimistic. In order to achieve his goals Stalin had severely limited freedom of expression in the Soviet Union. Wells met with his old friend Maxim Gorky and found that Gorky would not even listen to any disagreement about the virtues of communism. Stalin himself had revealed an absolute lack of concern about other nations, and a total lack of interest in Wells's vision of world government.

Wells left Russia disappointed. He could not know that his original perception of Stalin—as a tyrant, a dictator—was correct; he could not know that Stalin was responsible for death camps as terrible as those Hitler would construct just a few years in the future. Wells, ever the optimist, saw Russian communism as severely flawed but still holding some hope.

In England Wells once more was in the midst of several projects. One of them was the transformation of *The Shape of Things to Come* from novel into film.

Other films had been made of Wells's work. The first was a 1909 French version of *The Invisible Man*. In 1932 Hollywood produced *Island of Lost Souls*, based upon *The Island of Doctor Moreau*. The following year Hollywood produced *The Invisible Man*, starring Claude Rains. Both *Island of Lost Souls* and *The Invisible Man* were great successes, and both are still powerful films, frequently shown on television. These films, though, were produced by movie makers who simply purchased the film rights to Wells's books and developed the films on their own. Now Wells was asked to write a screenplay himself.

The opportunity to undertake a new type of communication was immediately attractive to Wells. He went to work on the film filled with enthusiasm and energy. He wanted to know everything about filmmaking and wanted to be involved in every aspect of the film's production, from writing the screenplay to devising special effects and working with the composer on the film's musical score. H. G. Wells, shaper of entire worlds on the page, was not about to pursue anything less when working on film.

His screenplay, *Things to Come,* was a distillation of his vision of the future. It was a grim portrait, and in some ways horribly accurate, as it told the story of Everytown, a typical English city. Everytown falls to the war that overwhelms civilization, war rolling forward in tanks, in aircraft, finally in great clouds of chemical weapons. There is total collapse; people living in squalor, strangers shot on sight.

Then, out of a sky that has for years been empty, appears a great and wonderful flying machine. Its pilot proclaims himself a member of "Wings Over the World," yet another version of the Open Conspiracy, this one composed of airmen.

The film's final scenes take place in the far future, in the magnificently rebuilt Everytown, a city of gleaming towers and technological wonders, a symbol of the new peace that has united the world.

But still there is dissent. The world is at peace, and some scientists wish to reach out, to launch men into space. Ignorance rises among the populace—the rocket means change, and they do not want the status quo disturbed.

Things to Come took two years to produce, and was released in 1936. Today, compared to *2001, Star Wars,* and *Star Trek,* the film appears quaint, even crude. But Wells's powerful vision and great storytelling abilities can reach even the most jaded viewer. The concern for the future works in the film's interest to make the effects more believable, the story more compelling.

If Wells's cinematic eye was cast upon the future, his pen carried him once more back into the past. In 1933, even as he was beginning *The Shape of Things to Come,* he was embarked upon another huge history. This time, though, the history book was not concerned with the history of the world, but only with the history of one of the world's citizens: the history of Herbert George Wells.

Wells turned to autobiography with the same enthusiasm for bringing new life to old forms that had made his novels so innovative, his essays so striking. In *Experiment in Autobiography: Discoveries and Conclusions of a Very Ordinary Brain (Since 1866)* Wells wrote a life story that is as much a story of thought and philosophy as it is of incident and character.

He began his autobiography with a statement of purpose. Life had grown confusing, he wrote, he was beset from too many sides by too many distractions. Wells wanted to come to an understanding of the way his "very ordinary brain" worked, and that understanding could be achieved only by writing about it. "I am writing a report about it—to myself," he began.

Experiment in Autobiography is candid and open. Wells writes as eagerly of his own shortcomings as he does of his many virtues. He slants, of course, many of his recollections to his own interest, but that is one of the purposes of auto-biography. He tells his story clearly and with many delightful side trips down avenues of memory and reflection. In the book the reader encounters Wells's family, his teachers, his love affairs and marriages, his growth as a writer and thinker, his friends, and foes, the Fabians, Henry James and George Gissing, theories of art, ideas, and insights. The book even contains an ample selection of "picshuas." There are photographs of his homes and friends, excerpts from books and articles, glimpses of world leaders. The book is as much a biography of its time as it is an autobiography of a man.

Wells completed *Experiment in Autobiography* during the final days of his visit to Russia. The book was published in 1934, just as work began on the film *Things to Come*. For many public people the writing of an autobiography serves as a capstone, a final gesture toward posterity, after which life is lived quietly. For Wells the autobiography was simply a way of getting his thoughts in order. He was approaching seventy, but he was not nearly through, not even close to a quiet life.

His plans for a Bible of Civilization still obsessed him, and during the late thirties he met frequently with scholars and publishers in an attempt to further the work he had begun with *The Outline of History.* His plans for his Bible grew even more grandiose. He saw now the development of an organized body of universal knowledge as an undertaking that could become an industry of its own: a bank for knowledge rather than money, a member on its own terms of the Open Conspiracy.

Audiences listened attentively to Wells's exhortations, but few members took action to make Wells's plans a reality. He found himself in the familiar position of prophets: He was listened to and then ignored.

Wells was a prophet, but he was not without honors. His seventieth birthday was celebrated with a tribute to him in London. Wells was moved by J. B. Priestley and the many other distinguished speakers who offered reminiscences and statements of respect. Wells's own speech was moving. He told of all his plans and projects with which he was aswarm. He mentioned, of course, his hopes for the unification of knowledge, for the brotherhood of mankind. But he knew that war was nearly upon the world once more, and there was melancholy in his reflection before the audience that while there remained much he wished to do there was little time in which to get it done.

Increasingly, after he turned seventy, Wells remained at his desk. He produced several more novels during the thirties, ranging from parables such as *The Croquet Player,* to scientific romances such as *Star Begotten,* to novels of ideas such as *Apropos of Dolores* and *The Holy Terror.* His books were often recapitulations of earlier themes, revisiting old ground, but they retained something of Wells's literary magic, and his intellectual youthfulness often sparkled through.

Nor was nonfiction neglected during these years. In addition to *Experiment in Autobiography* and the flow of articles, which were a constant and important part of his production, Wells continued to turn out books in which he set forth his opinions about the state of the world. His determination to make the world aware of the importance of world government was undiminished, his attacks on education retained their old fire, his visions of the future could still thrill and frighten. He was the future's first citizen, and he visited it again and again. Books by H. G. Wells appeared with a regularity that would be impressive for a young man.

But Wells was no longer young. He was entering the last act of his long life. His body was growing infirm, he was plagued with neuritis, his eyes were weak. And still he pushed on.

EIGHTEEN

END OF THE TETHER

DESPITE HIS YEARS, WELLS's temper could still be roused easily. That temper was lifted to angry heights in October 1938. On Halloween of that year the American actor and director Orson Welles dramatized *The War of the Worlds* over national radio. Welles's dramatization was so realistic that it inspired fear and panic among his listeners, many of whom did not know the program was a drama, but took it instead as a news report of an actual Martian landing and invasion. In England H. G. Wells was outraged that his work was put to such frivolous use, and for a time contemplated suing Orson Welles.

But there was a real war brewing and that prospect outraged Wells far more than any radio conflict. Germany had rearmed itself under the leadership of Adolf Hitler. In *Experiment in Autobiography* Wells had described Hitler as sort of a lunatic thirteen-year-old, obsessed, as Wells himself had been, with dreams of vast armies and world conquest. Hitler, though, was bringing those adolescent fantasies to life.

And H. G. Wells, aging, could only watch helplessly as Germany grew more and more bold, as war drew nearer each day.

When the war arrived it would be a bloody one. Wells feared that the carnage to come would destroy the world once and for all. He thought of the millions of deaths in World

War I and recoiled with horror at the knowledge that the weapons used in that conflict were toys compared to the weapons that would soon be brought to bear. Science had done its job: modern weapons were nothing short of devastating.

Still, so long as as he remained alive, Wells would do what he could to see that this new world war bore better fruit than had the last.

Even as the war was beginning, Wells sought to inspire debate over the sort of world that war's end would bring. If the aims of the Allies were not clearly spelled out *now*, he insisted, then the war would be fought, would end, and there would be won only a brief breathing space before war commenced once more. It was the endless cycle he'd presented so well in novels, nonfiction books, even in a movie. It was a cycle that must be stopped. Wells called, as always, for boldness: Let this new world war be fought to lay the foundation of a new world order, he wrote. Decide now that this actually will be a war to end all war.

Few listened. They had heard it before. As the war got under way Wells was seventy-four. To many readers he seemed to be a tired old man whose ideas were relics of another time. This was the *present*, they seemed to say, don't you understand that? Wells understood all too well. The first citizen of the future was trapped in a present that was just like the past —filled with people content, even dedicated, to taking the short view. Let's get through today: Tomorrow will take care of itself.

Yes, thought H. G. Wells, it would. It always had. More wars, more suffering, more ignorance, more death. He was a relic, all right. But he was a relic who had lost none of his inquisitiveness, that obsession with learning that had powered his career. In 1942, at the age of seventy-six, Wells became convinced that he needed to extend his academic credentials. He decided to seek an advanced degree in zoology. With that degree in hand, Wells felt, he might stand a chance of realizing a final dream. He longed to be elected to the prestigious Royal Society, under whose banner gathered the leading scientists of England.

Wells enrolled in London University, applied himself to study, and began writing his thesis. The thesis was entitled "On the Quality of Illusion in the Continuity of the Individual Life in the Higher Metazoa, with Particular Reference to the Species *Homo Sapiens*." Behind that long title lay a synthesis of Wells's ideas about the nature of human beings' individuality, and about the importance of collective effort to achieve the goal of a free, ordered, and peaceful world. All the old themes and concerns now presented in the form of a scientific report.

Wells won his degree, but he failed to win the recognition of the Royal Society. The society would not accept his credentials as a scientist. Having done so much for science in his lifetime, Wells was bitterly disappointed to end his life without membership in the professional organization he most admired.

All the while war raged around him. The battles grew bloodier each year. Hitler's forces dominated Europe. German bombers nightly rained destruction upon London. Wells's fears came true as technology served up increasingly destructive weapons, putting science in service to death.

Still more fearful devices lay ahead. Scientists for both the Axis and the Allies labored feverishly to perfect an ultimate weapon, a bomb that would unleash the destructive potential of the atom itself. Such a weapon would be equal to thousands of tons of conventional explosives. An atomic bomb would embody all of Wells's fears about the dark side of science.

And a portion of the development of this terrible new bomb would be traced to Wells himself. His 1914 book *The World Set Free* contained a fictional glimpse of an atomic bomb. Years after Wells's death, Leo Szilard, one of the developers of the actual atomic bomb, revealed that he had read *The World Set Free* the year before an understanding of the forces involved in a nuclear chain reaction became clear to him. Upon understanding those forces—an important part of the foundation of the bomb itself—Szilard immediately assigned his patent to the British government. As a result of reading H. G. Wells, Szilard wrote, he knew how awesomely destructive such weapons could be. Such power must rest only with responsible governments; that knowledge of how to manufacture nuclear weapons must never become available to the public.

Wells, of course, remained ignorant of the part he played in the development of the atomic bomb. He never knew of the effect his work had on Szilard. Perhaps he would have been flattered that he had persuaded one scientist to do what he could to protect the future of the world. Perhaps, though, he would have simply continued to feel disappointment at the yoking of scientists to destruction.

As the scientists struggled with the search for the secrets of the atom, Wells struggled with the end of his own career. Before entering London University he had published his last novel, *You Can't Be Too Careful,* which came out in 1941. Two years earlier he had launched his last major campaign, a struggle to have recognized a Declaration of Human Rights, which would set forth the rights that all humans, no matter what government ruled them, were entitled to. H. G. Wells's concern for human rights came decades before that issue would be made a focus of world attention.

His novelistic career over, his bid for acceptance by the Royal Society failed, his pen slowing down, Wells often felt himself near death. He still enjoyed meeting people and dined often with other writers. He and Rebecca West reconciled their differences, and for the last few years of Wells's life they were good friends. He met Somerset Maugham, Ernest Hemingway, George Orwell, and other colleagues. He remained in touch with his children. Richard Gregory, now Sir Richard, Wells's friend from Normal School days, was especially close.

Wells wondered often if he would survive the war. Would there be a world to live in if he did survive it?

His health was not good. He had developed diabetes; he had trouble breathing. He spent more and more time in his apartment. When Beatrice Webb died in 1943 he sent Sidney Webb a letter of condolence, expressing his happiness that their differences had been put behind them. Wells also remained in touch with George Bernard Shaw, and their correspondence both public and private remained filled with their antagonism to and fondness for each other.

When Wells did venture out it was for short walks through the rubble of London, walks that took him to the zoo where he observed animals going about their activities oblivious to the war. From these animals, Wells thought, had evolved humans. Where had humans taken a different path? Where had humans been caught up with the urge to self-destruction? There were no answers.

Despite the dangers of remaining in the city, which was the target of German bombs, Wells would not leave London. Many friends wrote and invited him to come to America to stay, but Wells refused. London was his home. He did not want it said of him that he fled simply because of physical danger. Besides, his home survived the blitz with only a single broken window to show for the Germans' efforts.

Wells still managed to get some writing done. He produced a variety of nonfiction books and articles, but they often seemed tired and bitter. His bitterness was genuine enough: The world was busy fighting a war he had predicted years earlier. No one had listened. How could he not be bitter? When asked what his epitaph should be, Wells's anger found voice: "God damn you all—I told you so."

Beneath that bitterness ran the strain of hope that had made him the spokesman for a generation. The world might appear doomed, but that was no reason to give up. So long as humans could draw a breath they could not allow themselves to be consumed by the darkness. Mankind must struggle to keep the light of hope alive for so long as even a single human spirit lived.

Wells's own light of hope remained the words he put onto paper. He marshaled his failing energy carefully, and with that energy managed a few final books. In 1944 he wrote an optimistic volume called *The Happy Turning*, in which he once more envisioned a glorious and peaceful world. In this slim book Wells was able to view the problems of the world as symptoms of a transition that mankind must make before it can obtain the happier world of the future.

There was one last book to write. It was a book that remains controversial to this day. Written in 1945, *Mind at the End of Its Tether* struck many readers as Wells's most bitter statement. Some even saw it as a repudiation of everything he had argued for in his life. The book was greeted as an essay in despair and hopelessness. Mankind is doomed, Wells seemed to say.

Mind at the End of Its Tether cannot be dismissed so easily. Wells's message was that the contemporary mind, the mind responsible for the sorry state of human existence, was doomed. Whether or not *Homo sapiens* survives the terrible dangers and challenges of the twentieth century does not matter. Something will replace us that can survive, and in that replacement, in a species more noble than ourselves, the mind of the world will at last find peace.

With that statement H. G. Wells's pen fell silent. He would pass the rest of his days watching, observing, looking for the light of hope.

On August 6, 1945, an awesome new light illuminated the world's troubles. On that day an atomic bomb was detonated over Hiroshima, Japan. All the new perils that confronted the postwar world were contained in the glare of that light. Wells reflected that nuclear forces could destroy all that was bad in the world—or all that was good. He would not predict which.

Out of World War II came the development of the United Nations, yet another attempt at a world organization. Wells played no part in this one. He was nearing eighty, and his days of striding the world stage were over. He had nothing more to say.

He had lived as full a life as any man of his time. He wrote more and better and more ambitiously on a wider range of subjects than any major writer of his time. He never wrote, perhaps, the one great book, the one great novel, that would stand as his artistic legacy, his masterpiece. But he wrote a shelf of books—more than one hundred—that taken together constitute an outstanding literary legacy.

Nor was he a writer content to separate himself from the world of which he wrote. He cared deeply about his world, sought to understand *all* of it, and gave his whole being to efforts to improve that world. He saw a future that could be bleak or bright, and worked for brightness. He had a great vision, and he shared that vision with everyone.

All his life he fought against war, and all his life he saw new wars erupt.

All his life he struggled to improve education, yet he knew that ignorance still outweighed knowledge.

All his life he labored and spoke and endeavored to tell his fellow beings that theirs could be a world of plenty and peace, yet a year before his death the most destructive weapon in history was unleashed.

All his life he *tried,* and watched as most did not.

He had done his best. It was for others to decide if that was enough.

Born in the year dynamite was invented, he lived a year beyond the atomic bomb. On August 13, 1946, H. G. Wells died quietly, alone in his room.

EPILOGUE

H. G. WELLS TODAY

NEARLY FOUR DECADES HAVE passed since the death of H. G. Wells. What is the state of his reputation today? What influence did he have on the world?

His fears that the human race would destroy itself with nuclear weapons have not yet come true. But there have been some frighteningly close calls, and the construction of such weapons continues unabated, although their number already may be counted in the tens of thousands. If there is a single issue that unites and galvanizes a wide variety of people in the 1980s it is the call for nuclear disarmament. In that call may be heard the echo of Wells's insistence that weapons too dreadful to use must simply never be used.

The world state, which was so central to Wells's thinking, has not come into being yet. The United Nations remains only a bare beginning for such a state. Increasingly rapid communications and transportation have "shrunk" the distance between nations. "Global village," a phrase coined by Professor Marshall McLuhan, refers to the disappearance of distance as a barrier between nations, brought about by electronic communications. Multinational corporations may, in some ways, be thought of as similar to Wells's Open Conspiracy of businessmen. But national boundaries nonetheless remain, international antagonisms still occur. True world government remains for future generations to develop and implement.

Education remains in disrepair in many ways, but there are some signs that Wells's concern for reforms in this field are at last being heeded. The example set by *The Outline of History* and Wells's other encyclopedic volumes has guided later writers and scholars in their preparation of texts that aim at universal knowledge—or at least at a broad foundation of knowledge—for the modern student.

Many of Wells's hopes about the improvements that science could bring about have indeed been realized over the past four decades. Time travel and invisibility remain unlikely, but space travel is midway through its third glorious and—so far—peaceful decade. Men have walked on the moon. A space shuttle is becoming a routine part of our lives. The probes that landed on Mars found no warlike Martians, but sent back something incomparably more valuable: knowledge.

Computers have been developed that greatly increase the speed with which humans are able to go about their business. The restructuring of life—so darkly presented in *The Island of Doctor Moreau*—has become a brighter reality through the marvels of genetic engineering; already scientists are developing new medicines, hardier plants, even beneficial organisms.

H. G. Wells's literary influence is easily seen. He remains in many ways the finest science fiction writer of all. In his romances can be seen virtually every great theme that science fiction explores again and again. Time travel, interplanetary war, space exploration, utopias and dystopias, immortality, invisibility, evolution, change—Wells refined most of these and invented some. It is common for a writer to go out of print after his death, or to be remembered for only one or two titles, but H. G. Wells's scientific romances remain in print year after year in a variety of popular editions. It seems likely that the scientific romances will remain popular so long as people read.

Not only Wells's themes, but also his methods of telling stories has had an effect on science fiction. "Realist of the fantastic," Joseph Conrad called him. That method, the treatment of the fantastic elements of a story as though they were to be taken for granted, was in many ways Wells's greatest gift to science fiction. Where earlier writers such as Jules Verne had gushed ecstatically over every speculation, Wells accepted change and innovation as a matter of course: His stories are about the effects of change on his characters and their world. That approach has been further explored and developed by the leading science fiction writers of modern times, from Robert A. Heinlein to Robert Silverberg, Isaac Asimov to Ursula K. Le Guin, Theodore Sturgeon to Barry N. Malzberg, and all the others who have helped make science fiction the serious and successful field of literature it is.

Science fiction writers are respectful of Wells's heritage; they know how much they owe him. One example may suffice for the entire field: the brilliant writer Brian W. Aldiss. An Englishman, Aldiss has paid specific tribute to Wells at least three times. In an award-winning novella, *The Saliva Tree*, Aldiss writes his own scientific romance of the nineteenth century, and gives H. G. Wells a walk-on part. Next, in a book of speculation, a worthy if more subdued successor to *Anticipations*, called *The Shape of Further Things*—whose title itself is a harking back to Wells's work—Aldiss explores many of the ideas that concerned Wells, and a good portion of the book is devoted to Wells himself. Most recently, Aldiss wrote a novel entitled *An Island Called Moreau*, in which he updates Wells's tale of the Beast People, and carefully reexamines for modern readers the themes that so concerned Wells at the beginning of his career.

Hollywood has not neglected Wells either. The 1950s saw the production of modern film versions of *The War of the Worlds* and *The Time Machine*. Recent years have brought productions that used Wells's name and Wells's titles but bore little resemblance to his actual work. It seems that the name H. G. Wells can still be relied upon to sell tickets at the box office; such a testimonial can be paid to very few writers, perhaps only Jules Verne and Edgar Allan Poe.

The most charming of all the recent films concerning H. G. Wells and his work was not based upon Wells's science fiction at all but upon his own life. This was *Time After Time,* a delightful fantasy that supposed that Wells actually constructed a working time machine and used it to pursue Jack the Ripper to modern times. The film is whimsical, a little foolish, very charming, and lovingly respectful in its attitude toward Wells.

Not only Wells's scientific romances remain in print. *The Outline of History* is still available, and has been updated more than once by scholars eager to make the book accurate in light of new knowledge. The scholars have also been scrupulous about preserving for readers Wells's original intentions.

Tono-Bungay, Kipps, and others of the serious novels are frequently taught in colleges and universities as examples of the influential and innovative novelistic work Wells accomplished. Like all good stories, the books are also still read for pleasure.

There is other evidence that Wells's legacy is a lasting one. His name is found frequently in the popular press, over quotes from his work or in examples citing his abilities as a prophet. H. G. Wells societies exist to help preserve his memory.

It is likely his memory would be preserved even without societies and college courses. Few writers exerted so huge an influence upon their times. H. G. Wells was in many ways petulant and egocentric: He never did understand that people and governments were simply not going to do things *his* way. At the same time that egocentrism was only one aspect of an extraordinary intelligence that was astonishingly perceptive about the directions in which the modern world was moving.

That intelligence was coupled with a great literary gift and insatiable curiosity, a combination that created sparks each time pen was put to paper. Wells believed in the perfectability of civilization, which may have been a foolish belief but which gave to his work a sense of urgency that is still clear today, long after the topical issues addressed have faded.

And, of course, he did not restrict himself to topical issues. A great deal of his work was universal in approach and appeal. He was not afraid of great ideas; he embraced them, examined them, and shaped them to his own vision.

It was a great vision, one of the greatest in the history of literature, and one that is still clear today to every reader who encounters the works of H. G. Wells and comes away seeing farther, knowing more, better understanding the world in which he or she lives, a world in many ways foreseen and influenced by H. G. Wells. He was a man very much of his own times, who speaks eloquently still for our own.

ACKNOWLEDGMENTS
AND
REFERENCES

H. G. WELLS'S LIFELONG concern with education was so deeply a part of his work that it sems only appropriate to begin a list of the references upon which I drew in the composition of this biography with a nod in the direction of the five finest teachers I have known. They are: Betsy Rogers, Dr. Eugene Pfaff, Dr. Richard Whitlock, Dr. Jerry Meisner, and Ted Reynolds. I hope that every reader of this book will spend part of his or her education in company with teachers as fine as these. They helped shape my own attitudes toward education and prepared me to appreciate the attitudes held by H. G. Wells.

While H. G. Wells felt frequent call to shout at editors and complain about agents, I've been much more fortunate. My thanks, then, to Linda Cabasin, a wonderful editor, and to Herb Katz, who first liked this book. And a special nod of appreciation to Henry Morrison.

As far as more scholarly references, there are several:

Experiment in Autobiography (New York: The Macmillan Company, 1934) by Wells himself is the one indispensable source for anyone desiring an account of Wells's life. Lively, opinionated, learned, angry, rude, funny—nowhere are the many sides of H. G. Wells better portrayed than in the pages

179

of this book. It is one of the great modern autobiographies and has been too long out of print.

H. G. Wells (New York: Simon and Schuster, 1973) by Norman and Jean MacKenzie is, simply, one of the outstanding literary biographies of recent years. It is well written, exhaustively thorough in research and representation, and places Wells squarely in a tradition of English thinkers and writers. The MacKenzies present a candid and complete biography of H. G. Wells that would be difficult to surpass. *H. G. Wells* is a model of what biography can and should be.

H. G. Wells: His Turbulent Life and Times (New York: Atheneum, 1969) by Lovatt Dickson is an engaging book that illuminates Wells's professional career. Much of the book's emphasis is on Wells's relationships with his publishers, and Dickson offers a fascinating glimpse of Wells as craftsman, artist, businessman, and world figure.

A book that will be helpful to the student seeking to understand Wells's critical reputation is *H. G. Wells: The Critical Heritage* (London: Routledge & Kegan Paul Ltd., 1972) edited by Patrick Parrinder. This book is a selection of reviews of Wells's work that appeared as his books were published. The reviews are fascinating reading in themselves and offer insights into Wells's changing status in the literary community.

An H. G. Wells Companion (New York: Barnes & Noble, 1979) by J. R. Hammond is a guide with thorough synopses and interpretations of Wells's novels, scientific romances, and short stories. The book contains a glossary to characters, titles, and locations in Wells's fiction.

Finally, there is no better way to understand H. G. Wells than to read—for the first time or the fortieth—his books. They are a monument to one of our greatest writers.

THE WORKS OF H. G. WELLS

H. G. WELLS's INCREDIBLE energy can best be revealed by a listing of his books. Many writers are prolific, producing dozens of books in the course of their careers. Most prolific writers, however, are either less than major writers or are writers who pursue a single form such as the novel. H. G. Wells was neither: he was a major writer who mastered virtually every form of prose.

This chronological list contains his books in order of publication but does not include countless articles, pamphlets, and position papers that Wells published in the course of his career.

1893

Textbook of Biology (nonfiction)
Honours Physiography (nonfiction written in collaboration with Richard Gregory)

1895

Select Conversations with an Uncle (literary sketches and stories)
The Time Machine (scientific romance)
The Wonderful Visit (fantasy novel)
The Stolen Bacillus, and Other Incidents (short stories)

1896

The Island of Doctor Moreau (scientific romance)
The Wheels of Chance (novel)

1897

The Plattner Story, and Others (short stories)
The Invisible Man (scientific romance)
Certain Personal Matters (humorous essays and sketches)

1898

The War of the Worlds (scientific romance)

1899

When the Sleeper Wakes (scientific romance)
Tales of Space and Time (short stories)

1900

Love and Mr. Lewisham (novel)

1901

The First Men in the Moon (scientific romance)
Anticipations (speculative nonfiction)

1902

The Discovery of the Future (speculative nonfiction)
The Sea Lady (novel)

1903

Mankind in the Making (sociological nonfiction)
Twelve Stories and a Dream (short stories)

1904

The Food of the Gods (scientific romance)

1905

A Modern Utopia (scientific romance coupled with speculative nonfiction)
Kipps (novel)

1906

In the Days of the Comet (scientific romance)
The Future in America (nonfiction articles)

1907

The Misery of Boots (nonfiction)

1908

New Worlds for Old (nonfiction about socialism)
The War in the Air (scientific romance)
First and Last Things (nonfiction)

1909

Tono-Bungay (novel)
Ann Veronica (novel)

1910

The History of Mr. Polly (novel)

1911

The New Machiavelli (novel)
The Country of the Blind and Other Stories (short stories)
Floor Games (nonfiction about miniature cities)

1912

Marriage (novel)

1913

Little Wars (nonfiction about war games)
The Passionate Friends (novel)

1914

An Englishman Looks at the World (nonfiction essays)
The World Set Free (scientific romance)
The Wife of Sir Isaac Harmon (novel)
The War That Will End War (nonfiction articles)

1915

Boon (novel in the form of articles by a fictional writer)
Bealby: A Holiday (novel)
The Research Magnificent (novel)

1916

What Is Coming: A Forecast of Things After the War (nonfiction)
Mr. Britling Sees It Through (novel)

1917

War and the Future (nonfiction articles recounting visits to the front)
God the Invisible King (nonfiction about religion)
The Soul of a Bishop (novel)

1918

In the Fourth Year (nonfiction about League of Nations)
Joan and Peter (novel)

1919

The Undying Fire (novel)

1920

The Outline of History (first volume of Bible of Civilization)
Russia in the Shadows (nonfiction about trip to Russia)

1921

The Salvaging of Civilization (nonfiction)

1922

Washington and the Hope of Peace (nonfiction articles)
The Secret Places of the Heart (novel)
A Short History of the World (nonfiction)

1923

Men Like Gods

1924

The Story of a Great Schoolmaster (biography)
The Dream (novel)
A Year of Prophesying (nonfiction articles)

1925

Christina Alberta's Father (novel)

1926

The World of William Clissold (novel)
Mr. Belloc Objects to the Outline of History (response to criticism of *The Outline of History*)

1927

Meanwhile (novel)
Democracy Under Revision (nonfiction)

1928

The Way the World Is Going (nonfiction)
The Open Conspiracy: Blue Prints for a World Revolution (nonfiction)
The Book of Amy Catherine Wells (tribute to Wells's wife)
Mr. Blettsworthy on Rampole Island (novel)

1929

The King Who Was a King: The Book of a Film (screenplay for an unproduced motion picture)
The Common Sense of World Peace (nonfiction)
The Adventures of Tommy (children's book)

1930

The Autocracy of Mr. Parham (novel)
The Science of Life (second volume of Bible of Civilization)

1931

What Are We to Do with Our Lives? (nonfiction)

1932

After Democracy (nonfiction articles)
The Work, Wealth and Happiness of Mankind (third volume of
 Bible of Civilization)
The Bulpington of Blup (novel)

1933

The Shape of Things to Come: The Ultimate Revolution (scientific
 romance combined with speculative nonfiction)

1934

Experiment in Autobiography (autobiography)

1935

The New America: The New World (account of visit with President Franklin Roosevelt)

1936

The Anatomy of Frustration (Wells's dialogue with himself)
The Croquet Player (novel)
The Ideas of a World Encyclopedia (nonfiction)

1937

Star Begotten (scientific romance)
Brynhild (novel)
The Canford Visitation (novel)

1938

The Brothers (novel)
Apropos of Dolores (novel)
World Brain (nonfiction articles)

1939

The Holy Terror (novel)
Travels of a Republican Radical in Search of Hot Water (non-
 fiction)
The Fate of Homo Sapiens (speculative nonfiction)
The New World Order (nonfiction)

1940

The Rights of Man, or What Are We Fighting For? (nonfiction)
Babes in the Darkling Wood (novel)
The Common Sense of War and Peace: World Revolution or War Unending (nonfiction)
All Aboard for Ararat (parable)

1941

You Can't Be Too Careful (novel: Wells's last)
Guide to the New World: A Handbook of Constructive Revolution (nonfiction)

1942

The Outlook for Homo Sapiens (speculative nonfiction)
Science and the World Mind (nonfiction)
The Conquest of Time (nonfiction)
Phoenix: A Summary of the Inescapable Conditions of World Organization (nonfiction)
A Thesis on the Quality of Illusion in the Continuity of the Individual Life in the Higher Metazoa, with Particular Reference to the Species Homo Sapiens (Wells's zoology thesis)

1943

Crux Anasta: An Indictment of the Roman Catholic Church (nonfiction)

1944

'42 to '44: A Contemporary Memoir (nonfiction articles)

1945

The Happy Turning (nonfiction/fantasy: Wells's dream life)
Mind at the End of Its Tether (nonfiction: Wells's last book)

INDEX